Pay It Forward Series

Notes to My Younger Self

– Volume 4 –

By Kezia Luckett
and Glenn Marsden

The Pay it Forward: Notes to My Younger Self. Volume 4

Copyright © 2022 Kezia Luckett

All rights reserved. No part of this publication may be produced, distributed, or transmitted in any form or by any means, including photocopying, recording, or other electronic or mechanical methods, without the prior written permission of the publisher, except in the case of brief quotations embodied in critical reviews and certain other non-commercial uses permitted by copyright law.

First Printed in United Kingdom 2022

Published by Imperfectly Perfect Publishing

Edited by Elise Abram and Daniella Blechner

Typeset by Oksana Kosovan

ISBN: 978-1-9163443-3-4

Praise for *The Pay It Forward series: Notes to My Younger Self*

'We each experience defining moments in our lives, moments in which we choose to drown in the darkness or look for the light, moments in which we choose to make our destiny or let our destiny make us.

This book is a collection of defining moments shared by some of the most inspiring and inspirational people in the world. It is a compendium of dark nights of the soul followed by sunny days of the spirit.

It is a lighthouse of sorts.

By spotlighting dozens of people who, like you and me, have experienced their own defining moments—"dark nights of the soul"—and found their way out of the darkness and into the light, this book provides solace, support, encouragement, and enlightenment for everyone hoping and praying for greener pastures and brighter days.

Each story in this book shines like a sparkling gem, sharing timeless words of wisdom from people who have known suffering, known loss, experienced defeat, and found their way out of the depths. These people have an appreciation for themselves, other people, and life that fills them with real peace, love, and joy.

These stories remind us that it's always darkest before the dawn, beautiful people don't just happen, and there is always a way up, out, or through whatever you experience... if you just hold on and reach out.

You might have seen or heard of some of these people before, and you might have discovered some of these gems on your own, while some people and their stories will be brand new.

In any case, as you read this beautiful book, you will be reminded time and time again that your pain can become your purpose, your self-disclosure begets others' self-disclosure, your confident vulnerability is positively contagious, and your happiness is your gift to the world.

If you or a loved one needs a little encouragement — some "chicken soup for the soul" — look no further. This book will uplift and inspire you to keep going, keep moving forward, and keep looking for the light within you.

So, don't walk — run to pick up your copy today. Then, you — like they — will remember that it's always darkest before the dawn, and only when it's dark enough can you see the stars. And you are that star! You are quite literally made of stardust.

As Elizabeth Kubler-Ross says, "When the darkness sets in, your true beauty is revealed... because there is a light within."

Rob Mack — Celebrity Happiness Coach, Author and Inspirational Speaker.

'This book, *The Pay It Forward series: Notes to My Younger Self*, is an empowering book with 12 unique, individual stories from some truly incredible and inspiring people.

This book demonstrates the potential that we all have. To dive deep inside our souls to find our true authentic selves, the theme of writing a note to our younger selves is beautiful. It allows the reader to see the inner work of navigating through challenges, struggles, and obstacles in life to overcome mental health issues and believe that it truly all starts in the mind.

From where one is today in one's journey of self-awareness, being able to love oneself for all one is, and accepting imperfections one believes are weaknesses that don't need to be fixed or corrected, comes spiritual enlightenment.

Paying it forward is the only way to impart this information to one's younger self. For those who have not yet tapped into their connection to self-awareness and the younger generation, this will give them a guide to learn the wisdom that will allow them to progress and upgrade their mindset faster without needing to face the challenges that have already been faced.

It doesn't matter what your "OLD" story was; the beginning is already written, and the ending is being written before your eyes. In your mind, it's time to rewrite the ending, creating a "NEW" story. How you decide to change the narrative in your mind is what matters.'

Sam Humphrey — Actor: The Greatest Showman

'The insight and wisdom from every person's story in this book is profound. Not only are there moments in which you see yourself in parts of somebody's story, but you also get to acknowledge how pain can be turned into purpose. There is something to be said about people sharing their vulnerability through their personal stories to demonstrate the healing process we all need to go through to find ourselves again. Thank you for this life-changing gift.

My own growing up was done in the public eye with over one billion people across the globe watching me weekly on *Baywatch* I lived out my highs, my lows, and my struggles very personally and made my mistakes, like we all do, in front of many. Yet nobody saw behind the TV screens, what was being written about me, and what was, in fact, my truth and reality. Where were all those people who watched the highlight reels of my growing up when it all fell apart? There was nobody cheering me on then.

These stories really hit home, and will help so many people navigate how to pick themselves up when the world seems like its crumbling and tap into that inner-strength, to keep going.

This book demonstrates that.'

Jeremy Jackson — Actor Baywatch

'This book is absolutely inspiring and unique. It gives true life stories that really help the reader feel as if they are not alone, uplifted, and that they, too, can have a great life despite any challenges. I highly recommend this book!'

Kim Somers Egelsee — Life coach, Author and Tedx speaker

Dedication

This book is for every human being who has looked in the mirror and disliked what they have seen. For every human who has been told that they were too much, too little, too loud, or too quiet. For those who have felt less than perfect whilst striving for the unrealistic goal of perfection. It's time to remember that we are all imperfectly perfect.

Contents

The Gift That Keeps Giving. **Blaine Bartlett** 31

You've Got This. **Chibs Okereke** 45

Lost Soul Wandering... **Ali Duggan** 61

Beauty & the Beast. **Aga Zielińska aka Skin Sensei** 79

My Sliding Doors Moment. **Clair Carrington** 99

My Choice to Fight. **Claire Gibbons** 113

Lame Ducks. **Esther Rowan Wells** 129

Every Moment, Every Choice, Every Experience Made Me Who I Am Today. **Kristi Maggio** 141

Rescued from Her Suffocating Shell in Hell. **Leigh Anne Gardiner** 157

The Lotus Self. **Romy Brooks, MSc** 187

Hanging onto Hope. **Tiffany Brix** 207

Why I Befriend Fear and Disrupt. **Somalía Brown** 223

Your Turn to Pay It Forward

In your hands you hold a book containing a wealth of hope, wisdom, knowledge and inspiration gained through the experiences of life.

To truly understand the power of the written word and what happens when people come together for a single cause, read the stories within these pages and, in the message box, write your own words of hope, wisdom, love and inspiration to the next person you are going to pay the book forward to.

Give it to a friend, family member, or even a stranger by leaving it on a bus, train, park bench, or even on the table in your local cafe. If leaving for a stranger, place a Post-it note on the front and write: "Yes, this book is for you. Read it. Love it. Pay It Forward."

Share Your Book & Pay it Forward:

Share a photo of you leaving or paying forward your book on social media on our official book page
www.facebook.com/ThePayitForwardSeriesNotestoMyYoungerSelf

Tag us in with these hashtags:
#payitforward
#imperfectlyperfectcampaign
#1billionlives
#aroundtheworld

Join us on our mission to positively impact on one billion lives

Pay It Forward Messages

Foreword

'One moment, caller,' I mutter to myself as I put my phone down and have to think about how to answer the question the lovely young man just asked me.

Twenty years ago, in school, I would have said, 'Just kinda going with the flow of life but looking forward to doing something meaningful,' but I can't really answer that currently. I'm supposed to have my life all set out and be successfully adulting.

School was prep for life. School was a wild jungle, survival of the smartest, street-savvy apex kids who got pretty much everything right, never doing anything they weren't already good at to risk looking weak, giving the impression they were awesome and definitely not worth challenging.

Back then, I was wide-eyed about life, hugely naïve, massively hopeful, afraid to 'get it wrong', and fueled with youthful confidence and ignorance. Guess what I ended up doing? Yep. Something meaningful. ☺

Going with the flow had me moving in the fast lane of life. Yeah, sure, I got caught in a few pond weeds that briefly held me back. I was fortunate to be sheltered by some great big tree roots, so I didn't have to weather those storms alone. All in all, my notes to my younger self boil down to going with the flow and having confidence, belief, and faith.

Don't get things twisted here: going with the flow didn't mean I had a smooth ride.

I went with so much flow I became flow (my state boundaries had no border control), emotionally battered by obstacle after obstacle (whoa—say that word more than once, and it feels weird) and my metaphorical juggling skills that, for sure, could get me into a metaphorical Cirque du Soleil.

My meaningful radar picked up a signal from Sydney that was a beacon to the world that it was cool to be imperfectly perfect. This was the moment I found myself doing something so meaningful it helped me feel like me again—the imperfectly perfect me.

What do you want to be when you grow up? I should have replied, 'Me.'

Where do you see yourself in the future? I should reply, 'Even more me.'

You can spend your most valuable young years in time trying to find yourself by adding, altering, comparing, and competing, seeking to improve upon what was designed to be left to grow into itself and reveal the imperfectly perfect person you are.

This book wraps up a powerful message into little bundles of self-love, a message that I wish retro-Rach had 20 years ago.

If only I knew that everything I was doing to get recognition in my effort to be perfect was me getting better at making things worse.

The making of me was, in fact, my breaking point when I could no longer hold everything together. Let's call it my 'making point'.

The authors contributing to *Notes to My Younger Self* have written a page upon page real guide to your own personal greatness. From breaking point to making point, the difference is the uniqueness of your Imperfectly Perfect Journey, and embracing that uniqueness with this book in hand is the first step on your best adventure: life.

Rachael Newsham
Health & Fitness Celebrity Coach

Instagram: Rachael_Newsham

Introduction

March 2020, like many others, will forever be etched in my mind. At that time, a series of events would forever change my life and the direction of the book series you hold in your hands, but I didn't know it back then.

In order for you to understand, I want to take you back to an event I was running just days before the world closed down. I remember walking into a large conference room that would be a home for women from around the world for two days as I hosted my annual "Destined for Bigger Things" conference, hopeful that the crew would have started setting up the stage.

Instead, I was met by one of our authors from Volume 3 who had flown in from Australia, saying, 'They don't want to start constructing the stage because they are not sure the event is going on. Please tell me I didn't get on a plane for nothing!'

As I approached the crew huddled around their phones, listening to the news, I heard the British prime minister trying to decide whether or not the UK was going to shut down.

The crew turned and asked, 'Do you want us to go ahead and set up?' to which I answered most definitely, 'Yes.' With women travelling in from Australia, Canada, America, Europe, and from all around the UK, we were going to spend some quality time at "Destined for Bigger Things" and celebrate the launch of Volume 3 of the *Pay It Forward* series no matter what.

For those two days, we were cocooned in the most beautiful space of connection, love, growth, and memories that would tide over many of us in the months that followed.

When the attendees flew back, many were put straight into quarantine in their respective countries. High from the energy of the weekend, we all figured it would just be for a short while.

In my own life, less than a week later, we would lose a family member to cancer, my father would move in with us, and we would enter into a worldwide lockdown, unlike anything the world had ever seen.

Through it all, I kept the faith that it would be for a short while and life would carry on as normal, but unfortunately, this was not to be the case.

It was at that point I had a heart-to-heart with God. I felt led to close down certain aspects of my business and put others on hold, including the *Pay It Forward* series of books. Through it all, I walked in faith and trust that He knew best, although I cried many a tear, hopeful that one day soon, this book and the vision He had given me back in 2016 would once again come to light when the timing was right.

Little did I know I would have to wait two and a half years, and there would be a slight change, even though the vision would ultimately remain the same.

The vision I was given back then was simple: to positively impact one billion lives by sharing stories of hope, wisdom, and inspiration surrounding moments of adversity.

Although simple, it seemed such a big ask when I was gifted it on a cold winter's morning in 2016. In fact, it sounded sooooo big and ridiculous to speak out loud that I battled with my ego as it constantly questioned who I was to bring this vision to light, who I was to think so boldly and so big, and who I was to think I could achieve the task.

But I learnt quickly as I shared with others what had been placed in my heart, and I saw them well up with tears in their eyes or give a shudder as they were covered in goosebumps from head to toe, that this vision had been placed in my heart for a reason, and that reason was to ignite something in others.

I was just the conduit, and I discovered that if I got out of my own way and shared with everyone I met from my heart, the right people would always step forward at the right time to share their own stories.

However — and I think it's important to add here — the collective mission to positively impact one billion lives has always featured YOU quite heavily. So firstly, thank you so much for picking up this book and getting this far.

The idea of this book is not only to pay forward stories of courage, wisdom, and inspiration from the most phenomenal individuals across the globe as they write back to their younger selves at pivotal moments of adversity but also to reach and touch as many lives as possible, so people know they are not alone, and this is where you come in.

At the front of this book, you will find a message box. This sacred space will allow you to add your voice to our mission.

Once you have finished reading these stories, you, too, can get involved.

In the message box, write your message of hope and inspiration to a stranger you might never meet. Once done, place a Post-it note on the front of the book that reads, 'This book is for you. READ IT. LOVE IT. PAY IT FORWARD," and leave the book where it will be found.

On a park bench, in a café, or even on a train, we know that the right people will pick up the book at the right time, and the message they will receive will always be what they need at that moment.

Back to the change in the direction God so beautifully placed in my path...Just under a year ago, I was introduced to a guy via Clubhouse, of all places. He was from the UK, living in Australia, and was also on a big mission. I won't go into his story as that is his to tell, and you will hear from him in a minute, but hearing his mission, 'The Imperfectly Perfect Campaign', and how it was changing the face of mental health by dismantling the stigmas associated with it touched my heart.

As a recovering perfectionist, I know that many previous authors, myself included, have been taught that our imperfections are the bits of ourselves we should try to hide, and that 'Perfection' is the benchmark for which we should strive.

However, as a Positive Psychologist, I know that when we fall short of this benchmark through our mistakes, failures, and adversity, we start telling disempowering stories. Helping people retell these stories has been my life's work for the past six years, and I know how much it has positively impacted people's mental well-being along the way.

When I got to know Glenn better, I realised that his mission and mine were so interlinked through the power of stories and the impact we were making that it made sense for the next volume of *Pay It Forward* to be a collaboration project.

With that in mind, we are so excited to share that *The Pay It Forward Series: Notes to My Younger Self* has come together for this edition with The Imperfectly Perfect Campaign to bring you Volume 4.

Before you hear from Glenn Marsden, the man behind The Imperfectly Perfect Campaign, I invite you to head to **www.kezialuckett.com/vol4/** to learn more about the courageous authors who have shared their stories within these pages and why they feel so passionate about making a positive contribution to the world. Thank you from my heart to yours for becoming a part of the mission that was placed in my heart so many moons ago to positively impact one billion lives worldwide.

Kezia Luckett
Positive Psychologist, Self-Compassion Consultant, Business Success Mentor and Creator of The Pay It Forward Series.
www.kezialuckett.com

The Imperfectly Perfect Campaign

I would have to say that it was June 2018 when something in me was set a light like nothing I had ever experienced before, and it didn't come from a great place.

In fact, it came from turning my social media platforms back on and news of the loss of an old friend from the UK being revealed to me.

You see, for me, social media was an old wound, a haunting reminder of something I had experienced several years earlier that, being honest, saw me dive deep, dark, and hard into a spiral in which I couldn't control my mental health.

Social Media, for me, was a vice.

At one point, it held me so tightly in its grip and stole my joy in life by comparing my behind the scenes to others' highlight reels. I took it further by comparing my body to those deemed 'perfect'.

Now, having experienced my darkest days, and thankfully, coming out the other side, I then experienced the loss of an old friend and found out it was due to poor mental health which led to him taking his life; the light I mentioned, hit me like a bolt from nowhere. It was like nothing I had ever experienced before, a passion, a drive, a calling from God, if you like, that knew I had to speak up.

I had to speak up for all the voices in the world of those who were silently struggling, voices that, based on societal expectations, feared that opening up would bring them shame and judgement.

It was this series of events that would change my life and the trajectory of my path for the years to come that saw me take the light that had been placed inside of me to the world.

The vision laid on my heart was clear, but the how wasn't so clear.

There I was with next to no experience in knowing how to get a message out around me, let alone to the world. I had no experience in how to draw attention to something that laid heavily on my heart, no experience in how it would be created, and certainly no experience in how I would move in a way to build enough momentum that it would help millions around the world.

That little voice of no experience came from a place that so many of us hold: BELIEF.

It is the Belief in ourselves, Belief in our abilities, and Belief in not letting our egos take over our minds that prevents us from even beginning a vision that has been placed in our hearts.

That 'vice' I spoke of was merely the detail of comparing myself to others, but when it all came down to it, the internal pain I was placing upon myself was something I knew I had to work on if I was to become the person I knew I had to be in order to get this vision out to the world, and that — like so many others — came down to Belief.

Yes, I masked so much, and the external implication for me personally was I took it out on my body and compared myself.

Why?

Because the Belief in myself wasn't there. I didn't believe that I looked good. The Belief that I was in the fitness industry and I needed to look perfect, and the more I tried, the deeper the lack of Belief I had in myself.

Though the implications of body dysmorphia went deep with emotional struggles, I fought hard and sought help.

It was the one thing that, as a man, we often find so hard to do.

Ask or seek help.

Another internal battle we face when confronted with the fact that we are not in control is that we don't know how to deal with these struggles.

The mind is a powerful source, indeed, and after seeking help, I realised that if the mind can take you to such a dark place, then it can equally take you to heights you could only ever dream of. The more we can work on removing all of these layers that have held us back for far too long, how we see ourselves, and the external pressures we put on ourselves, the more we can step into who we truly are.

I did just that; I finally released CONTROL.

I surrendered.

Surrendered to what I thought I had to do in order to get ahead, surrendered to being at peace with how God had made me, and surrendered to not thinking I had to be perfect.

In fact, I was going to lead by my imperfections.

As I walked this journey with the 'new' me and this huge vision that had been placed in my heart, my 'who I needed to be' was getting there slowly. My WHY was certainly there, but the HOW was still something I didn't know.

My journey has taken me further than anybody could possibly know, mentally, physically, emotionally and spiritually and let me tell you, learning to let go of outcomes, stepping out from your ego, and even surrendering to not knowing everything — simply put, the HOW doesn't always have to be answered.

Throughout my journey, the more I realised that visions are placed in our hearts by God, the more I leaned into a personal relationship with God, and the more I realised the vision placed in my heart had to be from a place of total faith, guided through intuition and ultimately BELIEF, that very thing I once lacked in myself.

Was I being tested?!

Total faith in the vision, total faith in being guided in the right direction, and total BELIEF in the person I was becoming throughout all the lessons of the journey were guiding me to become who I was meant to be so I could take it out into the world.

So, I did just that; I gave my full faith and Belief to it all.

I shared what had been placed in my heart with anyone and everyone who would listen. I poured it into others, and I walked each step of the path, one foot in front of the other.

My background wasn't in business, marketing, public relations, event management, or dealing within a networking capacity.

Through walking in faith, I stepped forward and learnt all facets of these areas. I led by humility and simply asked others when I needed help. Again, I led by my imperfections.

Most importantly, I used the gift God had given me: my voice. This is the ability to share my heart with others, and it resonated.

I also knew that committing to this; if I were to bring this vision out and create a movement, it would have to be led by the same footing of not being 'perfect'.

Chatting with a friend one day in conversation, I can say that God spoke through him on that very day and confirmed what had been laid in my heart by leading by imperfections.

...and thus, the Imperfectly Perfect Campaign was created. I was guided by faith, led to my friend through whom God had spoken, and the name rang so loud and clear. Not only that, it stuck, and it stuck in the minds of those who heard it far and wide.

Les Brown so rightly says that the story you are sat on, somebody is out there waiting to hear it.

...and many were ready to hear mine and so many others that I began sharing.

I reached out to some of those very people we often deem as unobtainable.

Celebrities, sports stars, corporate leaders, leading experts across the scientific and medical Fields. Simply put, I sent them a voice message through social media.

I didn't know what I didn't know.

I poured my heart out to them, sharing the vision that had been placed in my heart, and it began resonating, and scores of public figures started getting behind my efforts.

The vision God placed in my heart was starting to quickly form a movement in Australia, and messages commenced pouring in of the difference, hearing my story and hearing the stories of so many wonderful public figures across an array of industries was making to them.

It was opening up the hard conversations, seeking help, and saving lives.

With each step I made, with each step of Belief in my efforts and in where and what I was trying to do, the Belief in me got stronger by the day, as did how big of an impact I could truly have.

As I write this now, I graciously thank God for leading my path and placing this vision in my heart.

The Imperfectly Perfect Campaign has truly made an impact and continues to do so, not only in Australia but around the world. Now being featured in international publications and networks, it has seen over 450 of the world's most recognised and respected faces from all sectors sharing their stories, truths, and imperfections and is at the forefront of innovation when it comes to changing the narrative around Mental Health.

I was once told that by what God had placed in my heart, He was taking me further than I would ever know possible. He would open doors that no man could shut, and He would bring the right people with me along my journey to put more light out into the world and for humanity.

Well, He certainly put more light out into the world when I was introduced to Kezia Luckett and heard about the vision that had been placed in her heart and the impact she was and continues to make in the world with *Pay It Forward: Notes to My Younger Self.*

The more time we got to know one another and spoke openly about our journeys, the visions that had been placed in our hearts, and the more we knew God had brought us together for a reason.

That reason was to join forces for this volume and introduce not only women to the *Pay It Forward* Series sisterhood, but to get men to step forward too.

Glenn Marsden
Founder IPC Global, Success Mentor, Author and Motivational Speaker
www.imperfectlyperfectcampaign.org

The Gift That Keeps Giving

Blaine Bartlett

Leadership and Executive Coach, Bloomberg TV and Apple TV Co-Host, Best Selling Author, Keynote Speaker, Entrepreneur, Philosopher, and Consultant.

What are you passionate about and how are you contributing to changing the world?

I am passionate about transforming how businesses and business leaders conduct themselves. I believe that the purpose of business is to enhance the possibility of thriving for everything on the planet. Done well, profit will ensue. Unfortunately, for many, the purpose of business is too often thought to be the making of profit. It is not hyperbole to say that business is the most pervasive institutional force on the planet. There is literally nothing on this planet we call home that is not touched in some way by the activity of business. Because of the profit-centric focus of most business leaders, this activity usually and historically results in the calamitous degradation of the well-being of the whole. Make no mistake — business has a moral as well as a fiduciary responsibility to "take responsibility for the whole."

Therein lies my "mission" in life. I work with business leaders around the world to further their understanding and adoption of Compassionate Capitalism. This, as an economic model for ensuring that the workplace of today and tomorrow, allows individuals, organizations, society, and the planet the opportunity to thrive in a generative and sustainable manner.

Describe a pivotal moment in your life you wish to share.
It was my 12th birthday, and my mother sat me down for what she said was a very important conversation. That conversation, though seemingly innocuous to me at the time, proved to be a seminal event in my life.

I was what you would likely call a 'good kid,' but I was bored, and looking back, I couldn't quite put my finger on exactly why. As a family, we were lower-middle-class. As expected from his generation, my father worked diligently to provide, and my mom kept the home a safe and loving place for me and my siblings to grow up in. They had a strong marriage and were pretty solid role models. As a family, we weren't particularly religious, although my parents made a point of ensuring that we all attended Sunday School on a relatively regular basis. Their intent, as she explained to me, was to provide us kids with as complete an experience of their religious world view as they could. They both came from a relatively traditional middle-American Protestant background that, while not overtly fundamentalist, was still very steeped in doctrines of right and wrong, good and bad, and it was complete with images of hell and a judging, patriarchal God.

The gist of the conversation was that, as parents, they felt they had discharged their duties as it pertained to providing me with my religious education and—this was the big reveal—they knew that their worldview in this regard was limited to their own experience. They understood and appreciated that there was far more in this domain of life to be learned and experienced that they literally knew nothing about. This simple act of 'letting go,' of needing (or even wanting) me to conform to their religious beliefs, was nothing short of emancipating in ways I wouldn't appreciate until much later in my life. That simple conversational act—a gift, really—was an implicit invitation to explore and to question. It was an implicit declaration that they trusted me to act in my own best interest, and it was a catalyst that served to compel me to move beyond the accepted norm, to challenge the status quo, to question circumstances, and to risk stepping into the unknown with a developing confidence that all would ultimately be well.

Today, I truly consider that conversational 'gift' to be evergreen. It has served as a springboard that catapulted me out of what could be called 'common world thinking,' and opened doors I never knew or imagined existed. That simple conversation proved to be the impetus for creating a life fuelled by imagination rather than simply accepting a life dictated by circumstances. In the years following this 12th birthday conversation, I built a company with offices in four countries, touched the lives of over a million people, and learned to fly, scuba dive, ski, and sail. I've run a dogsled team above the Arctic Circle, run a raft down a river in Central Russia, flown aerobatics, meditated in a Zen monastery in Japan, explored the great religions, became an elder in the Masai tribe in Kenya, and have been called one of the World's Greatest Motivators. I regularly travel the world and have lived and worked in a number of different countries. I've written five books, including an international, number one best seller, with more to come. I became an Adjunct Professor at Beijing University and a member of the teaching faculty of the American Association for Physician Leadership. I was knighted by the oldest humanitarian organization in the world. More importantly than all of this, I learned how to learn, I learned how to question, and I learned how to live, all because of the simple gift my parents had given me on my 12th birthday.

Based on the wealth of knowledge, wisdom and experiences you have now, what would you have liked to say to yourself back then?

Hi Buddy,

Happy Birthday! It's going to be a fabulous year, and it is a year that will put you on your way to a fascinating life that you can't even begin to imagine today! These last 12 years have been filled with lessons you will only begin to appreciate much later in your life. These lessons will be powerful guideposts as you move waaaaayyyyy beyond what you or anybody you know right now can dream of. One of the more important of these is something you probably don't think of as a gift, but you will come to appreciate it as one of the best gifts you've ever gotten. It was Mom sitting you down the day you turned 12 and essentially saying to you that you no longer have to attend Sunday school, that she and Dad gave you access to what they knew about religion, and that they know there is much more...so go out and discover it. You won't appreciate the immensity of that gift for decades, but know this now: it will allow you the freedom to question, explore, and make mistakes, all of which you are going to be doing a lot of!

You can consider this letter to be a gift, as well, because I'd like to give you a bit of counsel around some of these early lessons that can, hopefully, make what you're going to be doing from this point forward a little bit less intimidating, although life will always be (until it's not) somewhat confusing, challenging, scary, and thrilling. To begin with, you've learned the true power of using fairness as a guiding value or principle. This began as a consequence of the closeness in age between you and your siblings;—the four of you were born within a span of four years—what were Mom and Dad thinking? This didn't leave much room for favouritism, and you learned early on that sharing was the best way to produce harmony in the family. Never underestimate the value of harmony...it makes a lot of things possible. Not the least of which is that it helps you know when things are becoming seriously out of sync, internally and externally. You will learn to pay attention to this, and you will use this a lot in your future.

Mostly, this will serve you well, but as they say, the overdoing of a natural strength can become a liability. You will want to start paying attention to something I call the 'For the sake of what?' If you're like me (joke), you won't really appreciate the power in this question until you're much older and start noticing that fairness and success don't always seem to go hand in hand. You'll have problems in business, you'll have a divorce, a couple of people will end up cheating you, and your wife of 20 years will die. None of it will seem fair. 'For the sake of what?' is one of the best questions I've ever discovered for keeping my head and heart in the right places. It's a question that's rooted in fairness, and at this stage in your life, you pay attention to doing things fairly because it feels right. You'll become more sophisticated about this as you live your life and experience some of what I just mentioned. You'll start to question if feeling right about something is always the best test for your actions and the actions of others. Hint: it's not. That's where the question 'For the sake of what?' comes into play. Used well, this question can cut through enormous amounts of bullshit. How you use this question will become one of your super strengths.

This leads us to another lesson I want to bring to your attention. Remember the two fights you had? One when you were five with 'Punky' Pasch, and the other when you were nine with Mike Sullivan. What I want you to know is that, while you didn't know it then, those fights were great examples of you figuring out early on that you could trust yourself to handle the consequences of a tough choice, whatever that may be. They were also great examples of you combining your innate sense of fairness with self-trust. You 'won' both fights, and you stopped fighting when your point had been made. You didn't press it further than it needed to be pressed. You respected both of them by not beating them. Remember this well because this becomes one of the ways you move through life. Beating the other person is not the same as winning — huge lesson, Blaine, and one that you will continue to develop and use as you grow older.

As you may suspect, some of these lessons go against society's notion of how success is supposed to look, notions like winner take all, get yours before it's gone, do what you need to fit in, don't look foolish, and what would others think? One of the big lessons that you will at times wonder and feel conflicted about is your streak of independence that is counterbalanced by not wanting to be left behind. Remember when you wandered off during the family camping trip to Crater Lake when you were eight? You were curious and followed your nose, and when you looked up, you noticed that the family car (and the family!) were nowhere to be found. You didn't know that Dad had simply moved around to the parking lot. All you knew at that moment was the scary feeling of being left alone, and you unconsciously decided, at the age of seven, that going out on your own could be dangerous. Blaine, you're going to take that decision you made when you were seven and use it to second guess and hold yourself back until you start your own company. I want you to know that there's good and bad news in this. The good news is that the decision not to get too far in front of your skis will keep you out of trouble when you're a teenager. The bad news is that it will become a blind spot for you as an entrepreneur that will result in your missing some great opportunities, but don't lose faith. That same blind spot becomes a perfect counterbalance to your not being seduced into copying parts of Dad's entrepreneurial zeal that sometimes got him into trouble. You will find a way to reconcile the yin and the yang of this and will create a successful company that eventually has offices in five countries.

That decision not to get too far ahead of others had a lot of reinforcement. Remember your first day at school? The students in the class were asked to count as high as they could. You learned to count when you were a toddler, so this wasn't a big challenge for you. However, you noticed the general range of the others' counting, and when it was your turn, you decided to stop at a respectable and acceptable 100 when you could have continued counting all day. Not overshadowing others was the fair thing to do, and holding back kept you connected. Why is this important to note? Because you are fast learning to recognize the value of connections. Your entire adult life will be organized around creating and maintaining high-quality relationships. You will have business clients and friends that will be with you for decades. Your attention to this will cause others to pay attention to it as well. It's how you become, for many, an exemplar of what we call Compassionate Capitalism. This is one of the ways you begin to discover why you're here on this planet.

You are a voracious reader, always have been and always will be. I know you started reading long before you were in school, and it was because of the exploration of other worlds, and other realities that reading made possible for you. This, too, is a part of your future. You are an adventurer and an explorer. Those long walks you take in the woods behind the house are more than your playing at being Daniel Boone. You're fascinated by discovering how nature and life work. Because of the way reading influenced and will continue to influence your imagination, you will soon begin to think about doing things no one in your family or peer group has thought of doing or being. You'll put together your first "bucket list" when you're 18 and will complete it by the time you're in your early twenties. It is one of the first clues that you can and must dream bigger! You will travel around the world in private planes, live in a number of different countries, learn to fly aerobatics and gliders, teach SCUBA, run dog sleds above the Arctic Circle, raft rivers in Russia, Japan, and South America, write many books, lecture to audiences of thousands, have your own TV show, be a professor at China's most prestigious university, be a millionaire and be broke, and personally touch the lives of over a million people. In your late twenties, you'll be doing a job that doesn't exist today. You will be one of the pioneers in what will become an enormous industry. Everything you have done and experienced up until now makes all of this possible.

Looking back, what made it such an important part of your journey?
This conversation was catalytic in the sense that it was the ingredient that provided the course change that transformed my life. It certainly wasn't a traumatic event as many course-changing events can be. It was a simple gift from another — my parents — that was graciously intended to enhance my experiences in life.

Subsequently, viewing my interactions with others through the lens of having the intention of enhancing life has contributed to my ability to work and live meaningfully and generatively in different cultures and has contributed immensely to my eventual championing of what I call Compassionate Capitalism. The invitation to question was embedded in this gift and became an important part of my understanding that questions are *always* more important than the answers. This understanding led me to question the purpose of questions. Moving from simply gathering information or trying to find an inviolate answer that would provide certainty, I learned to appreciate that questions determine direction. The question will always set the questioner off in a certain direction seeking an answer. This is the hidden power of questions: they set direction. Structured well, a high-quality question will move me or those to whom the question is posed into places they've never been before, which is the very definition of growth.

Additionally, my questioning of the purpose of questions also began to facilitate my questioning of what it means to be 'right.' Over the years, I've come to appreciate that the single most limiting and life-constricting phenomenon in life is our need to be 'right,' to have our beliefs about ourselves and our worldview validated. In my experience, I've come to the realisation that the overwhelming majority of people on the planet would rather be 'right' than have what they say they want. They seek certainty in a universe that is always evolving and changing. They want stability and safety when both are illusions, and striving for either is to desire a prison. Questioning is the antidote to this malaise, and it requires being willing to experience the extreme discomfort of sometimes having to change or transform myself and/or my worldview.

Learning to act on this realization began when my parents let go of their need to be 'right' about their religion being the one for me to use as a sentinel in life. Remember, questions determine direction; I've learned to stop asking 'why.' It's an omnidirectional question. It doesn't point in any specific direction. Rather, I've found that asking 'For the sake of what?' is a far more generative question. This question has become the bedrock of my work with clients. It is the question I use prior to making any significant decision. It's a question I used to discover my answer to the perennial question of 'What is life all about?'

None of us was provided with a user manual when we came into this world. The world—indeed, life—is agnostic as to what we want, where we go, or what we do. A part of the richness of the journey that began with this event is truly embracing that it's up to each of us to create meaning in our lives. Asked from a position of being interested in becoming everything I can be in the short time I have on this planet, 'For the sake of what?' is my go-to question. And it began to take root on my 12th birthday.

How did this event change your life?
The change this event produced in my life was gradual. It was literally an invitation to wake up to the possibility that life, as it appears, is not the life that could be if I were to activate and follow my imagination. Metaphorically, it was the equivalent of shifting the direction of my life one degree. At the moment of my 12th birthday, it was imperceptible. Over decades, the shift was one that literally moved me into other worlds and other realities. That innocuous, one-degree shift opened doors that, at the time, weren't seen,

possibilities I couldn't have imagined, and it provided me access to ways of thinking and being that was truly transformative.

What lessons did you learn?
The single greatest lesson I learned from this event is that the world and everything in it is a manifestation of a universal consciousness and that who I call 'me' is simply a vehicle that consciousness moves to and through. When I have felt blocked in life, it was always because I had begun to identify the results in my life with the 'me' I thought I was. I have come to appreciate that imagination is truly the gateway to that universal consciousness, and it is that consciousness that seeks ever-expanding growth and expression.

What would you tell other people experiencing this?
To take a bit of poetic license from a lyric from the movie MASH, 'Suicide is painless.' What I mean by this has *nothing* to do with physical death and everything to do with the *transformation* of my sense of self. One of the things I've learned on this journey is that what limits me is not who I think I am. Rather, it's who I think I am *not*! This event was in no way traumatic, and trauma is not a necessary ingredient for transformation to occur. Paying attention, staying awake, questioning, and asking, 'For the sake of what?' are all a part of creating a meaningful and fulfilling life. The simple truth is that if I'm not growing, I am dying. Growth doesn't have to be painful, and it is often uncomfortable. Contrary to how most people live, the world 'out there' does not determine what I have or experience in life. It's my internal world that needs attending, and I'm the only one who has access to that world. I must be willing to be uncomfortable in order to grow.

What are some of the things you would have changed about that situation if you could have?
I would have had a carrot cake instead of a German chocolate cake.

Any final words?
Genesis 50:20 says, 'As for you, you meant evil against me, but God meant it for good.' Nothing in this life is happening to me; it all happens for me. How I use it really does come down to 'For the sake of what?'

How can people get in touch with you and see the work you do?
www.blainebartlett.com

You've Got This

Chibs Okereke

Stress and Burnout Specialist, Mindfulness Expert

What are you passionate about and how are you contributing to changing the world?
I am passionate about reducing stress in a chaotic world. I have integrated ancient wisdom with modern-day science, turning them into practical actions to improve life in the present. I help my clients pull back the veil and get clear on their values so they can build an interesting, meaningful, artistic, and creative future, while maintaining awareness and gratitude in the present. I don't believe it's possible to change THE world; I do believe it's possible to change YOUR world. Once we realise that, we are free to choose our responses and attitudes in any given moment.

Describe a pivotal moment in your life you wish to share.
The year was 2016, and my entrepreneurial career was going from strength to strength. I lived in one of the most exclusive apartment blocks in Sydney, overlooking the opera house and the harbour bridge, with 360-degree views of the city.

I had a convertible Mercedes in my garage, a Rolex on my wrist, and I regularly travelled worldwide business and first-class in my tailor-made suits. I had dozens of staff across Sydney and the Philippines, and the companies I owned were turning over millions of dollars each year.

To an outsider looking in, everything was perfect. However, I had three very significant problems.

1. I was stressed.
2. I was depressed.
3. I didn't want to be there anymore.

2016 was my most brutal year. I was used to things working out for me. There had always been difficult patches in business, but I would simply roll my sleeves up, work three times as hard, and then come through the other side successfully. My luck, as I saw it, had finally run out. My company went from explosive growth to a massive death spiral within weeks. My usual resilience was nowhere to be seen.

Months of losing money, losing staff and battling with regulators left me mentally, physically, and emotionally exhausted. Despite the exhaustion, I couldn't sleep. I was cynical, detached from reality, and paranoid. I believed that none of my employees or partners cared about me or the business.

It felt like I'd lost 30 IQ points! I wasn't able to think clearly or make decisions like I used to. I would take drugs to get to sleep. I would wake up in the middle of the night in a panic with heart palpitations. It was an awful feeling. There was no light at the end of the tunnel, and taking my own life seemed the only option.

I remember rock bottom. How unfair is this world? A harsh, unforgiving universe tricks you into bringing new life into the world and then subjects that innocent child to the same horrors. If and when life gets too difficult to handle, one doesn't even have the option to 'tap out' because one has a responsibility to protect the child. What a cruel trick!

Time, recovery, and healing allowed me to realise that my daughter, Ziggy, was a blessing. She kept me present and grounded and gave me a reason to live despite adversity.

It wasn't the first time I seriously contemplated ending my life. The second time was amidst my burnout; the first was at the age of 11, staring at a kitchen knife, contemplating where to stab myself so that it would hurt as little as possible.

Looking back, what made it such an important part of your life journey?
My burnout in 2016 was the central turning point in my life thus far. I say 'thus far' because the world is constantly changing, and I know that life has one or two (probably more!) curveballs yet to throw at me.

In a previous section, I mention the fire that burns inside me and many others. I don't know where that fire comes from. Perhaps trauma, low self-esteem, genetics, or my soul's purpose—who knows? I've always wondered, and no doubt always will wonder, does one need to go through a traumatic experience to be truly present in life?

I look at that fire like a dragon. The dragon can fuel and energise us, or the dragon can destroy us. In my case, the dragon destroyed me, but this destruction was a gift.

In 2022, we are taking on more than ever. Many of us are in continuous hustle mode. We're putting time into networking, volunteering, stacking our kids up with extra-curricular activities, part-time studying, and working on our 'side hustles'. We are chasing 'success' in a way that simply doesn't add up. Most of us don't question where this idea of success came from. Still, I know that for the vast majority of my clients, when we dig deep into our motivations, we realise that we're following someone else's dream.

Burnout forced my hand and finally allowed me to focus on my mental health. It created space for bold decisions and new opportunities. Despite the internal voices telling me I was a failure if I quit, the fear of losing money, the shame, the anger, and the guilt, burnout outranked everything.

I had no option but to resign, walk away, confront the fact that I was miserable, and make drastic changes. I was forced to contemplate what really mattered to me. What were my goals? Was this how I want to spend my time? Was what I was striving for worth sacrificing my physical or mental health?

When we burn out, our cups are empty. We have no fuel left, so we do not have any energy to tolerate that which doesn't serve us. This gives us unique opportunities for clarity and allows us to reassess our values and priorities. We can, of course, choose to take a few weeks or months off and return to the behaviour that made us burn out in the first place, but that will eventually lead back to burnout.

Burning out gave me insight into what nourishes me and what depletes me. It gave me insight into what makes me happy and what doesn't. It allowed me to differentiate between short-lived pleasure and enduring joy. It helped me distinguish distraction from discomfort from long-lasting ease.

Although 2016 was my low point, I realised that I had been burning out for years, probably decades. The difference between 2016 and previous years was that I had expertly managed to ignore my stress symptoms in the years prior. During the period that I considered my 'good times', I now see clear signs of burnout. I would move from stress to chronic stress to burnout and back again. 2016 was the tipping point, the perfect storm of challenging events that drove me from burnout to habitual burnout.

It is still possible to recover from habitual burnout — I am a testament to that — but it is a far longer road to recovery. You will unlikely heal if you remain in your job and don't make significant changes. My goal is to help my clients recover from chronic stress and burnout before they reach habitual burnout.

Life often feels hopeless when we're burned out. Still, burning out and recovering has been transformational for me and countless others. Burnout helped me to let go of what was holding me back from living my best life.

Based on the wealth of knowledge, wisdom and experience you have, what would you have liked to say to yourself back then?

Dear Chibs,

Happy 11th birthday!

I'm going to tell you something you probably won't understand, but it will make much more sense as you get older. Not only will it make sense, but it will become your mantra and driving force in your forties and beyond.

Amor Fati.

Amor Fati is a Latin phrase that roughly translates as 'love of fate' or 'love of one's fate'. It is the practice of accepting, embracing, and perhaps even loving everything that has happened, is happening, and is yet to happen.

*The world is constantly changing, and **your** world is constantly changing. Without change, you wouldn't exist. Without change, no one you know would exist. In fact, without change, nothing would exist.*

Whether a change is 'good' or 'bad', whether it brings suffering or pleasure, whether it leads to gain or loss, change is necessary, and change is perfect. Fourteen billion years of evolution, metamorphosis, transformation, and change have brought us to this precise moment. Were it not for each universal event thus far, you wouldn't be here to read this, and I wouldn't be here to write this.

Have I lost you, little man? I promise you'll get it one day. For now, I want you to know that even though life feels hard at times, you are downloading some beautiful lessons, and you have a bright and wonderful future ahead.

You're a wise little soul, and I'm sure that, deep down, you already know this, but during those moments that feel too much to bear (and of those times, there will be plenty), I want to give you a sneak peek as to what you will be doing with your life.

Here are the highlights:

- *The worst period in your adult life will become your greatest triumph.*
- *You will be an inspiration to others and make a tremendous impact on the world.*
- *Hundreds of thousands of people around the globe will listen to your instructions at home, at work, in the car, and as they fall asleep.*

- *You will help people move through stress and suffering and save many from burning out.*
- *You will be a student of ancient teachings and take this bygone, often forgotten wisdom and make it relevant in the modern age.*

So, when does your journey begin, little man? At one point, I thought that your journey began in 2015 when you started to burn out, but upon reflection, I can see that it began long before that.

Do you remember when you and others were punished for sneaking out of the school grounds during lunch break to go to the candy store? Do you remember the wheels in your mind turning as it dawned on you that kids would rather risk Saturday detention than plan ahead and bring snacks to school? Do you remember discovering that if you bought things in bulk, you could charge more if you sold them individually? Do you remember being in the kitchen, making sandwiches, and packing your bag with the candy and soda you bought from the supermarket so you could sell them all at school for a tidy profit?

Your journey as a hard-working entrepreneur has already begun.

The lessons you learn at 11 will help you reach great heights. However, many of these same lessons will also help you burn out in a spectacular fashion. So, what advice do I have for you?

Amor Fati. Don't change a single thing!

Everything you are doing is perfect. Everything you are learning is ideal. All of your successes, challenges, sacrifices, heartaches, and failures will lead to opportunities you can't imagine. So please, keep doing exactly what you're doing.

I want to sincerely thank you for your hard work, perseverance through the darkness, and resilience. Keep your head held up; you are a special little boy and destined for great things.

I know you feel as if you've been dealt a rough hand. Your dad died when you were a baby, and the new dad that has recently come into your life hasn't made your life easier. In fact, he brought even more sadness and anxiety into your environment.

You don't get any hugs, kisses, warmth, or affection from Mum, and she offers little protection against the ritualistic violent punishments from your new dad. I know this hurts. However, this environment has moulded you into a fiercely independent, gritty, savvy, and self-reliant individual with the ability to control your emotions in the most challenging situations.

Your mum lives on government subsidies, using her single mother benefits to pay for you, your new brother, AND your dad. You are dealing with the shame of wearing second-hand clothes and handing in your free lunch voucher at the canteen when everyone else pays with cash. I know you wish you had more, but the scarcity you're currently experiencing will inspire you to find unique and fascinating ways of making money. It will make you ever so grateful for the abundance that you receive in the future.

You were clever enough to get a scholarship to a private boarding school, but your primary school headmistress told your mum you would be a 'bad apple' in a private school, so Mum decided it best not to take the opportunity. You might feel like your Harry Potter moment has been sabotaged. Still, through the public school system and remaining at home you will develop a quick wit, street smarts, and the ability to live on the edge without getting into too much trouble. Those smarts will get you out of many sticky situations in the future!

*You look different from the black kids, you look different from the white kids, and you think differently than everyone. You're reading **1984** and **Brave New World**, and you ask your teachers for extra homework. You're extremely tall, you stand out, and you have a strange name. You are unconventional and unusual. Even though you wish you were just like everyone else, I promise that, once you get older, everyone will compete to be different, and people will marvel at your uniqueness.*

Your dad constantly tells you that you are not good enough and that being a black kid in a white world means you need to be twice as clever as everyone else and work three times as hard. You'll be happy to hear that the chip on your dad's shoulder didn't transfer to you. However, this constant negativity will manifest itself as a strong work ethic. Once you trust that the universe has your back, your diligence, hard work, and perseverance will allow you to achieve great things.

Your dad lives in a delusion. He calls himself a businessman, but to this day, he has never pulled off a successful deal. Almost 40 years later, your dad believes the 'big multimillion-dollar deal' will finally be pulled off. Although you resent him for it now, you will learn to admire his tenacious optimism. Believe it or not, you have inherited your optimism from him, the determined belief that one will eventually succeed with hard work and determination. Ironically, and in his own way, he is the perfect model for perseverance and never giving up.

Your dad exaggerates his success, makes up stories about his education and sporting past to impress others, and pretends to be someone he isn't. I know you're beginning to see through the charade, but I want to tell you that his unusual behaviour will shape you in remarkable ways. In an effort not to follow in his footsteps, you will cultivate the ability to see the truth and cut through delusions. Also, to distance yourself from this behaviour, you will develop humility and a self-deprecating humour that allows you to connect with others and put them at ease.

I come to you with a conflict. Although it might sometimes feel as if you have a cursed life, you will become enormously grateful for the challenges you have faced and have yet to face.

I could give you advice. If you follow it, your life will become much more manageable. However, if you follow my advice, you might not gain the wisdom and fortitude from battling adversity.

Through deep work and mindfulness, you will reach a point in your life where you will realise there is absolutely no rush. Events unfold at their own pace in precisely the right way. That is why I have decided not to give you any advice.

I could give you all the answers now, but I know you like to work things out for yourself, so who am I to deny you all of these incredible lessons yet to come? In my experience, there are two excellent ways of learning. The first is battling through adversity, and the second is learning from your mistakes.

There's no rush.

Your life is going exactly as it should.

Amor Fati.

I have a few things to tell you; please remember these through the dark times. The most important thing I want you to recognise is that **everyone is doing their best with the tools they have.**

Currently, you believe you are not loved by those whose job is to nurture you. At times, you may even feel hated by them. You will be shocked to discover that someday in the future, Dad will apologise for everything he did. He will tell you he loves you. He will tell you he tried to toughen you up for a dangerous world. He will tell you stories about his childhood that will fill you with compassion. Of course, this does not justify his actions towards you. However, his childhood trauma certainly explains it.

I also want to acknowledge the fire inside you. You don't yet have the right tools, so that fire will eventually burn you out. That fire will feel like anxiety or angst for much of your life. However, you will soon realise that the same fire is the birthplace of creativity, and when it is managed effectively, that fire will energise, warm, nourish, and elevate you to great heights.

You don't have to burn out to do extraordinary things, but you'll work that out yourself in good time.

There is one more thing I want you to take away with you, a quote that will inspire you later in life.

'Everything can be taken from a man but one thing: the last of the human freedoms — to choose one's attitude in any given set of circumstances, to choose one's own way.' — Viktor Frankl.

*You cannot control what happens to you in life, little man, but you can **always** control how you respond to what happens. There is magic in that unique and uncomfortable space between what happens and how you respond. Choosing your response is the ultimate freedom. You will soon learn to stop exerting control over the world and begin to take responsibility for how you view the world and respond to it.*

With Amor Fati, you can change how you perceive your place in the world. Is life tough? Great! How will this challenge allow you to grow? Have you experienced loss? Fantastic! How will this loss help cultivate gratitude for what you have? Are you burning out?

Amazing! What self-reflection can you do, and what doors are now open to you?

A negative attitude will not change the past; however, an optimistic attitude can help improve life right now, at this moment, and what is life except for a sequence of moments? And if we can string together positive moment after moment after moment, we can create a general sense of ease, calm, well-being, and perhaps even occasional glimpses of peace.

There's no rush. Everything always works out, and we get there in the end. Enjoy the moment, little man. Enjoy the simple pleasures of life while you can. You only have one life — WE only have one life — so try not to take it too seriously.

As Carl Jung once said, a man grows with the greatness of his task. You've got an enormous task ahead of you, little man. Godspeed!

How did this event change your life?
I've always had a strong work ethic, but with the misguided notion that the harder and longer I worked, the closer I would get to where I wanted to be. My burnout allowed me to course-correct and move in a new direction, one that gave me purpose and aligned with my values. Firstly, I had never taken the time to define my values, and my burnout gave me that clarity. Secondly, I now have healthy tools that I can use to manage my stress instead of unhealthy tools (alcohol, drugs, social media, and chocolate!!). My new tools help

me get on track faster, nourish rather than deplete me, and I can now get more done with less stress in less time!

What lessons did you learn?
I've learned so many lessons since my burnout. These are my top five:
2. There is no rush; events unfold at their own pace.
3. Attitude is everything. We can't control the world; however, we can control how we respond to the world.
4. Humans have a thirst for simplicity, yet life is complex. Nothing is black or white, right or wrong. The more relaxed and mindful we become, the easier it is to let go of judgements and be comfortable in the complexity.
5. Life is uncertain. What is certain is that there will be challenges ahead. We can spend all of our time planning to avoid adverse outcomes, or we can spend some of that time training to be resilient in pain or discomfort.
6. Don't take life too seriously. We're not here forever, so enjoy the game.

What would you tell other people experiencing this?
Burnout can often feel unbeatable, never-ending, and with no light at the end of the tunnel, but this sense of being overwhelmed is a signal, not a life sentence. I am talking from intimate experience, both my own experience and that of my clients. Burnout can have severe consequences if left untreated. However, once we bring awareness to the signs and causes of burnout and implement the right strategies, the harrowing experience of burnout can be a turning point, a stimulus to launch you towards a happier, healthier, more sustainable life. I'd say career, but I mean life.

What are some of the things you would have changed about that situation if you could have?
I would change absolutely nothing. Everything in my past has led me to where I am today, and I wouldn't want to be anywhere else.

Amor Fati.

How can people get in touch with you and see the work you do?
www.chibs.co

Lost Soul Wandering...

Ali Duggan

Mental Health Pioneer and Life Magician, Actor, Speaker and #1 Best-Selling Author

What are you passionate about and how are you contributing to the world?

I dream of a world where poor mental health is no longer judged or pitied but treated with compassion and understanding. As the saying goes, there but for the grace of God, go I.

I am passionate about people not suffering in silence and that no one should feel alone. I show others there is another way to heal from pain. My greatest wish is that no one endures the heartbreak of another unnecessary loss of life.

I am working on various creative projects, both in a performance capacity and behind the scenes. I am a storyteller at heart, sharing my stories and those of others to deepen an awareness of life's struggles and develop empathy, making the world a happier place to live for all.

Describe a pivotal moment in your life you wish to share.
My life began to take a different turn about four years ago. Before that, I was running from crisis to crisis, and my health, both physical and emotional, had become severely impacted. I lived the kind of life where I was always on the go, not making time to rest, always finding something else to do or someone else to help but never making time to stop, look after myself, and simply be, not showing myself compassion for my failings, whilst offering it in bucket loads to everyone else, but most importantly, blocking out trauma, which lay festering deep within my body.

I disregarded the warning signs and treated my body with disrespect. I've received comments on my high pain threshold (something of which I'm very proud) — someone once even called me superhuman. Yet, for me, I considered my body like a machine, to be fuelled with food, water, and exercise to function efficiently, but it was scorned when it didn't look right or wasn't working the way it should. I ignored the splutterings of the machine until, one day, the machine broke!

Two years earlier was my *annus horribilis*, with six family bereavements, including that of my mother-in-law, interspersed with hospitalisations for a twisted colon and being treated for vasculitis, an auto-immune condition. I continued to work through all of this, except for when I was arranging and attending funerals, juggling hospital appointments, and when my hospital admissions quite literally forced me to stop. Well, not exactly... I was still making phone calls regarding another person's care from my hospital bed. Though my physical body was out of action, my brain was in overdrive.

Finally, I had a massive wake-up call. After a crazy 18 months of episodic flare-ups, debilitating pain leaving me unable to eat without anti-spasmodic medication, and three hospital stays, my surgery turned out to be life-changing! My body was cleansed and free. I was eating without pain and without concern for the consequences, which was a novel and much-welcomed experience. During my extended time off work, I decided that it was time to stop putting my life on hold and do something. Anything.

I'd had a dull ache inside me for years, telling me that I wasn't fulfilled in my life, but I didn't honestly believe I could do anything else or be anyone else. I wasn't unhappy as such, more frustrated that others were moving on in life whilst I trailed behind.

My search led me to the Energy Alignment Method, an experience like no other. Through this work, I cleared unmasked trauma and blocks keeping me stuck and manifesting as social anxiety over many years. Then, two years ago, I discovered sound healing. It was perfect for me as I'd always used my voice to process emotions through song. Little did I know that this would be the start of a whole new level of shedding the many layers of my past.

Looking back, what made it such an important part of your journey?
In many ways, this chapter in my life felt like a grieving for and a rebirthing of the part of me lost to trauma. The acknowledgement of pain in all its deep, raw messiness was the start of my healing

process. For the first time ever, I dropped the front, and I actually reached out for support from friends and admitted that I was not okay. I was no longer blindly soldiering on alone; I had two trusted friends by my side, and for that, I am eternally grateful.

I have changed so much since then. You see, I was living an incongruent life, one that was always concerned with being kind towards others, yet I could be so cruel to myself at times. I had spent years avoiding the challenging parts of myself and my past.

I was curious to know more about Complex PTSD through my role as a Mental Health First Aider, so I read up on the symptoms, and I realised that they described me perfectly. Suddenly, it dawned on me: the many faults in my character were a reaction to trauma. The inability to truly relax, the avoidance of particular situations, the overreaction to criticism, the constant hypersensitivity to sights and sounds, the living on standby, the underlying feeling of being unsafe, and the constant need to be safe — I felt as if I'd been metaphorically running away for most of my life.

If I had known this earlier, I would not have berated myself as much for my shortcomings. When I became aware that I had been suffering emotional flashbacks through most of my adult life, in a strange kind of way, I felt normal again.

Psychologically, this was the scariest period of my life, with flashbacks that transported me back years in time. I'd had flashbacks before, but this was on a whole new level. I wouldn't wish that experience on anyone, although it has given me a deeper understanding of how powerful they can be. Whilst everything on the outside looked normal, inside, my world felt like a ticking time bomb had just exploded. I wandered around in a daze, but I knew I had to confront it once and for all.

I clung to the fact that I'd faced my fears before and come through. Even though. at the time, I had no idea how, and it felt as if the pain was never going to end, it was only by being honest with my inner anguish that I could set myself free. Once I had lifted the lid on that pain, there really was no way back. I needed to acknowledge it, feel it, heal it.

So, in my darkest times, my biggest breakdown was my biggest breakthrough. Now, when I have a moment, when something unsettles me and threatens to tip me over the edge, I know, deep in my heart, that something is waiting to be unearthed and worked through. Every day I feel like a stronger, happier, and more confident version of myself. That's because I'm always true to myself, and that's a wonderful place to be.

Based on the wealth of knowledge, wisdom and experience you have now, what would you have liked to say to yourself back then?

My Dearest Alison,

I can't believe you're speaking so openly about what's going on for you, but you can't contain all of this pain any longer. It's spilling out everywhere. You're under a doctor's consultation, and it's time to step up and own what happened. It's not your fault... It's not your fault... It never was!

Everything tumbles out, the things you wanted to say and the things you can't stop yourself from saying, and then you hear him mention a sick note, and suddenly, something inside you snaps, and the fighter in you emerges (that's always been there deep within).

'What do you want on your sick note?' he asks.

'PTSD,' you reply.

He seems surprised. 'Are you sure?' He checks.

'Yes. It's PTSD, so that's what's on the sick note,' you reply adamantly.

It's time to close the door... No, not in the way you thought. Finally, it's time to release the chains of your past, for I have to tell you that the pain you are going through right now gets so much better. It teaches you so much. You're stronger than you think, stronger than you know. You have always seen yourself as weak, but you're one of the strongest women I've ever known.

It's time to start the process of letting go. To allow yourself to heal...

Secrets and shame.
Guilt and blame.
Keeping you trapped
In sorrow and pain.
Let's find the chink.
Let your light in.
I'll hold your hand,
So, shall we dig in?
I'm always there,
For every stage.
To help you release
The bars of your cage.
You have the key.
It's right by your side.
To be your True Self,
There's no need to hide!

I know you're hurting too much to believe me, but it's true; it's actually true. You believe that you are your pain. That's because you're broken, not in a way that needs fixing but broken from circumstances that are outside of your control.

You are not your pain.

Your pain is a consequence of what happened to you, and you're doing everything you can to survive. You are more than surviving—you're shedding the layers of pain like dead skin. You're living life!

Do you remember watching that film, the one about suicide and the pain of those left behind? That's the reality. You might think that no one would miss you, that no one could love you, that your very existence is pointless, that you are pointless, but it's not true. You are loved more than you'll ever know. What will it take for you to see this, to believe this? You are worthy of all the love that is coming your way.

You've reached out for help — that's the first step. It's not the solution; that comes much later in life.

You will be so proud of the woman you have become. Shall I tell you a secret? She was always there, hiding, waiting patiently for her opportunity to shine. If only you had learned to trust her sooner...

You've started writing poetry again, like when you were younger. It's not so light and fluffy as it used to be, but you're a grown woman now who has experienced life and all its curveballs.

Losing your spark.
Sat in the dark.
Secretly crying,
Inside you're dying.
Head is exploding,
Bombs are imploding,
Insides corroding.
Despair, yet don't care.
The day has come.

The time is now.
There's no way out...
You don't know how.
Then something stops you,
There's someone to tell.
A way to escape
This living hell.

There are joyous times; there are challenging times ahead...

University will feel like a time for reinvention, a time for new adventures. It didn't work out exactly as planned—that's quite an understatement! In your second year of study, you are involved in not one but two car accidents in the space of four months, both dealt with in your own unique style.

After the first, you were affectionately called 'Hop-along', although perhaps 'Rock-along' might have been more apt. You mastered your crutches with ease (despite blisters on both hands) and were often seen using a lengthy swinging motion to manoeuvre yourself quickly across busy town roads. Oh, the irony, the excitement of being in your first shared house... with an attic bedroom. You didn't see that one coming!

Heaving yourself up and down two flights of stairs on your behind, making your own way to lectures, fighting against gravity up a huge, steep hill—it was draining, but it makes me smile now just thinking of the absurdity of it all. Finally, common sense kicked in... Not before time. Treated like a VIP with your very own taxi service (the university maintenance team), who also took you to your numerous physiotherapy appointments.

Little did you know this wouldn't be your first time on crutches or your second or even your third: once after landing awkwardly on the pavement (no, you weren't drunk); then, after falling down stairs during pregnancy (pelvic girdle pain ensued); next, after bowel surgery (you were too weak to stand unaided); and finally, your most recent escapade (hopefully, your last one), during breast cancer treatment.

Anyway, that did have a happy ending. You've now had the one-year all clear. There's much more I could tell you here, but I'll leave that for another time.

You are a warrior!

It will feel so good to be back on your feet again. Hooray! Yet on the first day of the Christmas vacation, contented after a day of present-shopping, you will hear a car zooming behind you whilst walking back along the country road home. You turn, dazzled by its headlights coming towards you, and stop to let it pass, but I hate to tell you this: it will be too late. Suddenly, you will find yourself on the ground, screaming (you won't remember how). Still, it could have been so much worse! At least you scared them enough to seek help before they sped off into the distance, leaving you by the wayside.

Your parents will arrive home to a note from your brother. They will have already seen the ambulance outside of the nursing home but not thought anything of it. They just assumed there had been another incident. They will follow you to hospital. Upon seeing their distressed faces, you will (in your usual manner) quip something, this time about your mum's facial lines.

'Well, you put them there,' she will reply.

'Do you need painkillers?' the medics will ask.

'No, it's okay. I've still got some from my last car accident. Oh, I could have brought my crutches back,' you joke with a wry smile.

Your first injury limited your mobility for some time, and you'll suffer regular pain flare-ups for years but it will be your second car accident that will leave its indelible imprint of trauma. Initially, head and neck injuries will mean that even resting your head on a pillow will cause you excruciating pain. However, the nightmares and flashbacks will be the hardest to bear. Nonetheless, you will still soldier on.

So, why am I telling you this?

You see, you have a wicked sense of humour that you use to make light of any situation. You have a crazy streak inside you. Believe me, it doesn't always end well! But that's what makes you you. It's when you lose your sense of humour that you are truly lost. If you can dig deep and find that within you, you'll be just fine. Now, when I say fine, I don't mean nothing untoward is ever going to happen again. That's unrealistic! But you'll always find a way through, though, no matter what.

That's your Superpower!!

Because, in spite of it all... losing both grandparents within a year... painful periods and haemorrhaging leaving you bedbound (or should I say bathroom bound)... a real possibility that you will never have children... despite financial constraints... somehow, you manage to gain a degree. It's not the result you hoped for, but it's a degree, nevertheless.

Busily catching up on assignments whilst revising and taking exams, going right to the wire... your tutors won't think you'll make it, though thankfully, they only tell you that later. Somehow, with sheer grit and determination, you will do it. So, don't go beating yourself up about being a 'failure'. What does that even mean anyway? You did this yourself. You succeeded against all odds.

If you saw who you are today, you simply wouldn't believe it. You're amazing! Know that you can achieve anything you want in life. Hold onto that stubborn streak, and never give up! Whenever you find self-doubt creeping in, remember that you might stumble, but you will never fall.

You have nothing to be ashamed of.

One of your heaviest burdens for too many years will be that of shame of the past you can't leave behind. You see, you made the choice to live, yet you will carry these darkest times close to your chest, locking away the pain and throwing away the key.

So, life was brighter.
Well, the pain subsided.
Buried at the bottom
Of a bottomless sea.
No place for hope.
No room for joy.
Going through the motions
Like a wind-up toy.

Secrets, secrets, so many secrets...

I know all of your secrets, everything you sought to hide for fear of rejection. The ones you are clinging to, even now. The ones borne out of physical and psychological trauma, the self-destructive patterns and self-sabotaging behaviour — I know all of this, and guess what? I still love you.

Your unhealthy relationship with food, veering from comfort eating (as a way of self-love) and then not eating (punishing yourself) — I know the reasons behind this, and I forgive you.

Food was your coping mechanism, a crutch propping you up when life seemed overwhelming.

There's no need to walk alone. A trouble shared is a trouble halved, you know...

Will you let me in? I can show you the way if only you could release your tightly clenched jaw.

It started when you were labelled overweight during puberty and continued as you tried but failed to fit into your petite sister's clothes. You didn't realise then about body types, how the only way you could ever be that size was if you were unwell.

When you fall pregnant, you won't like the way your body changes, how it expands, the way it makes you feel fat, the feeling that your body is out of your control, and the disconnection with your body at what should be the happiest time. You will measure your waist constantly during pregnancy, then weigh yourself at the earliest opportunity upon arriving home after giving birth. You will despair at not being able to fit into your pre-pregnancy clothes. I feel sad even writing this...

So much pain, it's easier to block it out; or so you think. It will just come back to haunt you in a myriad of ways. Weaved in a tangled web, you can't find a way out by yourself.

Breaking down barriers, piece by piece,
Watching my outer shell crumble.
Feeling the pain,
Bleeding inside.

The storm behind the calm.
Pain patiently waited its turn,
Pain bursting through barriers
Until the light could shine again.
Not hiding any more...
Not hiding from who I was meant to be.
The best is yet to come...

You're in a much happier place now you've learned to unpack it all. Like Humpty Dumpty, you're putting yourself back together again, finding the parts of yourself that have gone AWOL.

Your resilience is unbelievable; how you deal with everything that life throws at you with a bucket full of perseverance and a sprinkling of good humour thrown in.

You're you now, not in spite of these circumstances, but because of them. You're sharing your story to benefit others. 'A shining light' and 'an inspiration to all', that's what they're saying. Yes. About you. Would you have ever thought that possible? You always thought you had nothing to say—how wrong you were!

You no longer hide huge parts of yourself; it's a bit like always having to have the best china on display, but it's exhausting, isn't it? It sucked the life out of you for way too long. Because when you're so busy trying to be perfect and everyone else is busy doing the same, you lose connection, and that's the most important thing: connection, love, and self-compassion.

Wherever you are,
Wherever you go,
You're so much stronger
Than you even know.
Leave the past behind,
Don't look far ahead,
Just live in the now…
For you're too long dead.
Take all the lessons,
Use all the learning.
Don't ever give up,
Just keep on yearning.
Stay true to yourself,
You'll find peace within.
Why are you waiting?
It's time to begin!
Love yourself always
In times good and bad
But never forget
It's okay to be sad.
Look for the best things
You'll find all around.
Let go of control,
Life's treasures abound.

Striving for perfection is just wasted energy. Strive for brilliance, maybe, but never perfection. Don't ever compare yourself to others, for they are on their path, and you are on yours.

Always remember that your life is a journey, not a race... and promise me you'll have a lot of FUN along the way!!

Yours always, in love and laughter,

Ali x

How did this event change your life?
For the first time ever, I prioritised my mental health above and beyond anything else. I sought help, and now I no longer use diversion techniques to escape from reality. But most importantly, if I had not faced trauma from previous life events, I would not have had the strength to deal with my next significant challenge... breast cancer. My diagnosis came only six months later.

What lessons did you learn?
I learned to gather all my troops around me to help me fight when I felt too weak to do so. A simple heart emoji or funny meme on my down days was so powerful. Just knowing someone was thinking of me, even if they felt helpless, helped more than they will ever know.

Only through this deep explorative process have I connected the fact that body image and visibility are inextricably linked in a dichotomy between wanting to 'look good' versus the fear of the 'unwanted attention' that may bring. This has held me back in so many ways. Now I know that it is only by loving myself and my body as they truly are that I can achieve inner peace.

What would you tell other people experiencing this?

Please do not try to struggle on alone. We all need to ask for help sometimes. When I am weak, you may be strong, and so the cycle of life continues. Allow others to be there for you and be there for them, too, but always remember to put on your own life jacket first!

What are some of the things you would have changed about the situation if you could have?

How I wish I'd been more honest with myself and those closest to me sooner. Because of the shame around my feelings of not being able to cope, I only spoke my truth to therapists. If I had shared with loved ones, I would have realised that my inner torment was a normal reaction to trauma, so it turns out that I was not that weird after all.

In my need to appear in control of life, I actually unwittingly pushed people away because they couldn't relate to me. I was like a swan swimming serenely on the surface whilst paddling desperately underneath. Now a massive weight has been lifted. Others notice it, too, and I'm a much happier person to be around.

Any final words?

It is always possible to turn your life around. I'm living proof of that! Trust in yourself and take that one first step. I promise you: you won't regret it!

How can people get in touch with you and see the work you do?

https://linktr.ee/alicduggan

Beauty & the Beast

Aga Zielińska aka Skin Sensei

One & Only Skin Ekspert™ in Poland, on a mission to set your skin free from fake perfection pressure. Author of game-changing skincare system Skin S.E.N.S.E.I.®

What are you passionate about, and how are you contributing to the world?

If I ask you, 'how would you rate the satisfaction from your skin (from one to ten)?' what would be your answer? Do you like your skin, the way she looks? Note your answer; we will get back to it a bit later.

Yes, I use the word 'she' when I speak about skin, and I treat her as a live person because, during the last eight years, I realized how strongly the look of our skin influences our self-confidence, our mindsets, and our self-care. Our skin can be like our BFF (best friend forever) or our WE (worst enemy). Whatever emotions the skin brings, she plays a massive part in our lives, and she deserves to be 'her.'

Yes, you've guessed correctly—skin is my passion.

For years I've been obsessing over and researching everything connected with skin and skincare, and really, what's missing in the market. I've realized that our approach to our skin and skincare is wrong, and I've decided to change it. That is how Skin S.E.N.S.E.I® (Scientific Evidence Navigation Strengthening Epidermal Integrity) was created: a skincare system discovering the skin's needs, starting with genetic and epigenetic conditioning, finding a 'why' — the real cause of why the skin 'behaves' like that, and what processes need to be fixed by which ingredients, ending with tailor-made skincare routine based on an individual's time and budget.

The aim is simple: to change our attitudes toward skin and skincare.

What is my mission?

Let's follow the first question, to which I've already heard over 10,000 answers, and I have had only one 'ten' Usually, it's around 'five' or less.

What was your note? If you gave your skin nine to ten, I'm so proud of you! But if your answer was between one and eight, let's follow it with another question: 'What would have to change to have your skin be a solid nine?'

Your answer becomes my mission.

Describe a pivotal time in your life you wish to share.
Surprisingly for you, my reader, it was not my skin that made me feel 'not beautiful enough'; It was my body. I was not slim enough,

and it was difficult to control, causing an endless struggle for the 'perfect result.'

I needed to grow up in my forties to understand how colossal impact this struggle was and how the emotions caused by it had impacted my entire life. The funny thing is that I wasn't fat at all, and I didn't have weight issues either (at least from a BMI point of view). It was my 'control-freaking brain,' seeing my body in a different mirror than it should. Why? Well, I believe I became an 'ideal beauty' beast victim.

To understand this situation a little more, you need to know that Poland was closed to the Western world until the nineties. The former Soviet Union's dependence after World War II impacted our history until 1989 (Okay, it still has an impact, but that's another story). We didn't have open and broad access to Western culture, colorful magazines, and all the trends that were there at the time. The citizens of the Western world had the chance to get used to it through time; I didn't. I still remember the first *Cosmo* edition in Poland (1997). It meant something new to me, and I still have it.

Suddenly, in 1990, we saw the wonderful, shining life of rich American people (*Dynasty* with Joan Collins) with all of their sparkling clothes, jewelry, and make-up. We all wanted to have it, but our options were still limited. Information, trends, and images were abundant, but at the same time, we could hardly buy anything like that. We could find imported clothes of all colors, sizes, and fabrics, yet it was so chaotic and difficult to manage for a teenager who wasn't really a fashion fan. We were learning to live in a world of a completely different shape, and that was also the time I had to start growing up.

The changing body of a teenage girl resembles the 'Ugly Duckling' rather than the 'Beautiful Princess.' It is usually pretty evident for everybody except for the teenager. I remember one situation when I was going to buy a new pair of jeans. There was a market (there were no commercial centers yet, or at least, of the present type) with different things: clothes, accessories, lingerie, and shoes. I wanted a pair of dark green jeans. There was only one style (even if there were more, I wouldn't have the slightest idea which one was for me). Despite the many years (30 to be exact) that have passed since that event, I still remember the moment when it became apparent that I needed to wear jeans two sizes larger due to my rounded hips and very slim waist. The fashion at the time did not appreciate women's curves, and this prompted a completely different pattern. I felt so ashamed and humiliated that my body did not fit into the right size. All of the joy of shopping disappeared and was replaced with shame, a dislike of my body, and the determination to change it.

At the time, no one said, 'There is a problem with this pair of jeans. You should just try a different style.' Instead, I heard, 'You need to lose some weight because your hips are too wide for the trousers.' They weren't—I know it now—but this one outing affected my entire life later on. I spent years trying to have control over my body, to make my body fit in the correct size from top to bottom (the bottom = the hips).

I lost many years fighting with my body, trying to make it perfect—not in function but in appearance. I lost years feeling guilty, sacrificing, permanent dieting, trying to rationalize food, to control it, and in my mind, I was losing the battle. I couldn't make my hips slimmer despite trying so hard.

And so, as a young woman growing up, I fell into the trap of correcting something that never needed any fixing. For many years I tried to strive for an unmatched ideal.

I spent so much on magazines, books, and CDs that were supposed to give me the perfect dream body. I smeared myself with all sorts of cosmetics to get rid of cellulite and followed many diets, including laxative herbs.

Yes, you might be right: I was dangerously close to both anorexia and bulimia.

The beauty industry had clawed its way into my life. In this aspect, it became my Beast, fed by my fears, frustrations, and the quest for unattainable perfection.

I let the industry created to make me feel beautiful take away my strength, take away my confidence, and take away a part of me.

It took me years to understand that every single body is different, and everybody is unique.

Working in the beauty industry, dealing with skin care products, I noticed which mechanisms affect clients, how commercial and marketing campaigns are created, and how the message is crafted, and I began to understand what had influenced the teenage me.

I accepted the shape of my body being in my thirties, but I still know how to feed my Beast, and I sometimes do, although the events of recent years (insulin resistance, Lyme disease) have taught me to be gentler with myself and take care of my body for health and not imaginary beauty.

Working with clients and their skin, I've seen similar behaviors. The quest for perfect skin without a blemish, without a single enlarged pore or blackhead, causes young women to lose sleep. On the other hand, I've felt the frustration, shame, and anxiety of women having severe skin problems (acne, rosacea, atopic dermatitis). They felt stigmatized. They covered their faces with the strongest make-up to avoid mean comments about their skin and appearance.

I really believe that we can stop this, and I believe that we can show our beauty as it is. Let's stop feeding the Beast.

Looking back, what made it such an important part of your journey?
I didn't exactly realize this event was crucial until I recalled it. I would say that my whole life, especially its business part, was supposed to bring me to the point I am right now. I was working with clients, taking care of their skin, healing it, and teaching about the cause of their problems. Still, I needed to return to my emotions connected

with that event to realize that there was a more significant cause: the beauty industry itself, the Beast.

This made me think, and I've noticed a pattern. From an early age through puberty into adulthood, every woman—every person—is introduced to the prevailing canon of beauty. In the case of skin, it is supposed to be smooth, pleasant to touch, full of radiance, and without imperfection; Just FLAWLESS. We do everything to attain this unattainable beauty. We feed the Beast with our emotions, frustration, fear, anxiety, and lack of confidence, giving it power.

I needed to face my emotions and my perception of my body. I needed to deal with it to be ready to change the world's perception of the skin and its attitude toward skincare. It was a healing process for me.

Based on the wealth of knowledge, wisdom and experience you have now, what would you have liked to say to yourself back then?

Dear Aga, or should I say Dear 'Green,'

As a teenager, you will grow up in a time when Claudia Schiffer, Naomi Campbell, and Cindy Crawford are considered the most beautiful women in the whole world. They are the ideal of beauty, perfect women. Every teenage girl will want to look like them with their perfect bodies, perfect hair, and perfect skin.

Colorful magazines and new TV commercials will showcase the direction every teenage girl should follow, and this will be the start of generations fooled by the idea of what perfection means, not that you know this now.

It doesn't mean that the idea of being good-looking or beautiful wasn't present in girl talk before the nineties, but as you know, the eighties in Poland were rather grey — multiple different shades of grey, in fact, but still grey. Martial law in 1981 and everything following this event left a mark on that part of our lives.

No one gave much thought to this aspect of our lives because there weren't many resources for it. There was no pressure to be perfect. There was no pressure to shine and sparkle like the heroes of **Dynasty** *with Joan Collins. But as the nineties come in and the shift happens in Poland, your life, little Aga, will suddenly seem like a world full of juicy, Technicolor stuff. Now, you won't be able to stop it — in fact, you will get swept away by it — but it's not your fault as you won't have developed your defence mechanisms against the pressure under which all young women will suddenly find themselves.*

Like many other teenagers, you will follow the new beauty world's message by buying books and colorful magazines (no social media yet), practicing new skincare tips, trying new makeup products, and experimenting with your hair.

You will soon know that beauty is not only for the body but also for your hair, nails, and skin, and they change from time to time as the beauty industry wants women's lifelong interest and attention from the beginning of their lives to the end.

You have an advantage. Your skin is flawless, the color of 'milk with a drop of blood,' as your mother's friends described it, even though you feel embarrassed with your skin because it turns red and reveals your emotions; it is like your skin is betraying you. You feel the heat in your cheeks, which stresses you out even more. However, your skin is not the issue for you but your body.

You are growing up in very bizarre times in Poland, Aga. Before 1989, there were not many clothes shops. You weren't so interested in fashion (and you will not be), but also, as a child, you weren't interested much in fashion and stylish outfits.

After 1990 and in later years, the whole country will be flooded with many different types of clothing of various brands, styles, and colors. It will be around this time that you start reading **Cosmopolitan** or **Shape**, and you discover that 90:60:90 is the most desirable shape for every female body.

In that one minute, your brain will need to adapt to all of the information from the last 20-30 years from the Western world. That will be, and still is, confusing for you as you absorb so many new ideas, information, and issues.

On top of that, there is a paradox. Taking care of yourself, of your beauty, is treated as vanity, a waste of time and money. What matters is education and achieving success. A job, an apartment, *or a car is the goal for every young person. 'Put your education first because you will not find a good job in the future,' everyone says. Skin or body issues are not the most important things. After all, you can cover them up with makeup or clothes.*

I know that you will struggle with your body at ages 13, 14, and 15 as your shape and look change, which becomes so annoying. Your waist is still so thin, and your hips are becoming wider. You are becoming a young woman. People (mostly men) will start to see it; they will comment on the fact that you already have breasts. It's true. It will be humiliating to hear them joke and comment in a very suggestive, sexual way, and you will not feel strong enough yet to tell them to back off. Instead, you will learn how to show a poker face, to hide your vulnerable 'you' deep inside.

Sadly, there is no one you can talk to about it. Your mum and sister are not emotionally open to talking about femininity and sexuality, and it is a taboo subject, and not only in your family. NO ONE knows how to talk about the body, sex, and beauty in Poland at this time.

Your mum and sis don't feel your problems as they have entirely different bodies. In their eyes, your body is normal. You are healthy, not fat, so only sometimes will you hear some 'good advice' like 'don't eat too much if you want to stay slim.' Your family doesn't know that you will feel every comment like that as a bullet that hurts and determines you to try to become even more perfect.

You have genetic conditioning from your dad's side, and he is always on a diet, but you don't compare your body to his but to other women's. That is probably why you decide that you will do anything not to look like his sister, your aunt (who you will name 'a three-door closet' because of her extensive hips).

You will soon learn how to hide your emotions, and how to react to any comments about your body, how not to show that it affects you. You will pretend to be indifferent and confident, but inside, you admit that you don't like your body.

In the future, as a Skin Ekspert, you will know precisely how your clients feel about their skin. You will understand their emotions, not only because you are an empath but also because you've been there.

There is another thing I need you to know, understand, and remember. You have rare skills and a rare personality type that makes you see the world differently than your teenage friends, colleagues, or even the adults in your life. You just know things, you just feel things, and you know more. Also, be aware that it's not that easy to be an introvert in an extrovert's world (especially when they cry louder, and you often know that what they scream is not correct or it is just stupid). They will assume you are shy, but believe me, they are wrong. You just need to think of what you want to say. Sometimes, you don't want to say anything. It is and will always be your choice, and you don't need to explain or feel strange about it, but yes, unfortunately, you will feel like you don't belong.

You don't know yet, but you will work in the beauty industry. In the beginning, for beauty corporations, then for your own company. Your own business will start with a meeting with your friends in which you will hear many questions about skincare: 'Aga, I found this cosmetic product with these ingredients—does it work? Is it worth it?' 'Aga, you know this stuff—tell me how to take care of my skin. Tell me what to use—I'll do anything you say,' and so on.

Deep inside, you will feel that their words don't mean that they just want more information about cosmetics or ingredients. They feel lost in this whole 'beauty world.' They need guidance, and they need to find someone who will take the responsibility to tell them how to take care of their skin, how to keep their skin healthy, young and beautiful, and how to choose from the large number of cosmetics that is offered to each of us, and how to personalize their skincare routine.

That is how the Skin Ekspert project will begin, with a unique approach to skin.

You will think it will be so simple. In the beginning, you will be convinced that you will work with clients who want to prevent their skin from aging (just like you), but you will be wrong. During your first meetings outside of Warsaw, you will meet so many young women with acne, rosacea, problems with excessive dryness, as well as reactivity or atopic dermatitis.

However, it will be Anna who will significantly influence your understanding of your future mission. She will say these game-

changing words during her skin diagnosis concerning repeatedly appearing acne inflammations: 'I feel so ashamed with the look of my face that when I go to the kindergarten to pick up my children, I hide my face because other people look at me and judge me. I hide my face so nobody can see it.' She will cry, and you will hug her.

At that moment, you will understand how much the appearance of the skin affects the perception of self, and how much it disturbs people's self-esteem and self-confidence, how much each of us wants to feel appreciated, comfortable, and at ease in this world that values superficial beauty.

You will dig deeper, and during many hours of self-education, you will understand that where there is a result (issue), there is also a cause. The reason 'why'. As in Newton's third rule, the action causes a reaction. There is always a cause for skin problems and every move made and every cosmetic product put on the face will generate a response from the skin.

You will start searching for the principal cause of every skin problem, and you will find out that there is a lack of epidermal integrity (I know you won't understand these words now), most commonly known as a destroyed skin barrier, but when others (beauticians, beauty, and skinfluencers) say, 'Skin barrier is important, so take care of it. Use product X to restore it,' you, in contrast, will say, 'Restoring your skin barrier is essential to making your skin healthy as it is the starting point for every single skin issue, including acne, rosacea, seborrheic dermatitis, atopic dermatitis, dry skin, brown spots, sensitivity, and wrinkles.'

That is how and why you create your skincare Skin SENSEI® (Scientific Evidenced Navigation Strengthening Epidermal Integrity) system, and you will start to educate and guide women (and men) on how to treat the skin as a system of interconnected vessels, each of which affects the other, and a disruption of one can cause a skin problem in another area.

With this approach, instead of masking the symptoms of damaged epidermal integrity, you will match the necessary active ingredients to the needs of the skin's barrier to solve its problems from the starting point.

During your eight years of work, you will develop this system by 'adding the feelings', healing the emotions, and giving hope for better skin. You will keep your promises, and it will be a game-changer for thousands of Polish women in their journey to enjoy their skin again.

This work will also be a part of your healing process, but that is still in your future. Right now, let me tell you something really important: you are absolutely gorgeous. There is nothing wrong with your body. Actually, when I look at photos of you from those years, you look stunning and phenomenal!!

It was the trousers' cut and style problem, and not your body!

You are so lucky because you don't need to be paid attention to be perceived as beautiful. You don't need to wear makeup or spend time preparing yourself to go out. Your skin is an object of jealousy. You look younger — okay, I know it's not what you want to hear when you are a teenager, but you will appreciate it after 40, believe me!

Thanks to my words, I hope you will start to love yourself (the whole you) more and more, step by step. You don't need to control your body. Take care of it, and give yourself love and appreciation because you deserve it. And your body deserves it, too.

I know you don't want to be seen as pretty because people often say that, 'a pretty girl is a stupid girl,' but please look at who is saying these words around you. It was mostly your father and other people with emotional issues.

As for your dad, let me explain one thing to you: your dad wanted (and still wants) you to be intelligent, educated, and wise because he wanted (and still wants) a better future for you. For him, being the best was a goal. It was the only way he could stand apart from his siblings. He was a middle child, and he showed his uniqueness, intelligence, and skills to feel better than his siblings. Then, his parents became interested in him, and that's why he forced you to be better than others.

Unfortunately, he does it maliciously, forcing you to fight him for your dignity, for the right to be yourself, for the right to disobey him, for the right not to listen to sexist comments as they hit on you and your mom's femininity, for the right to be intelligent because your mom is stupid, worse, hopeless. It is his issue. He fears strong, intelligent women because they might be better than him. Again, this is NOT YOUR PROBLEM!! You are not him, and you are not like him.

As for the others—and you will meet many of them, believe me—they have emotional issues. Just tell them to 'back off' any time you hear that you can't be pretty and intelligent.

So, hear me out, my dear teenage Agnieszka: you are a beautiful woman who is intelligent, bright, has unique skills, and can change the world by being herself. You are brilliant and beautiful being a woman, feeling a woman, and not being ashamed of your sensuality. On the contrary, be proud of it. You are perfect just the way you are. There's nothing to improve in you.

I know it's a lot to digest, and you still prefer some rules, so below you will find my rules for you to make you feel happier :)

1. *Like and love yourself; don't be harsh.*
2. *Your body and your brain are two parts of you. They are both beautiful and valuable and need your love and care.*
3. *Don't control everything you do. Don't control your body—it's so exhausting.*
4. *Food is just energy for your body. Good food is something you can enjoy without guilt. When you learn to show your emotions, you will not need food to comfort you.*

5. *Make yourself happy (whatever makes you happy: books, music...) at least occasionally.*
6. *Don't listen to others saying that you should do this or that (unless you value their opinion—you will eventually find these people).*
7. *Don't put too much pressure on yourself. You don't need to be perfect in what you are doing.*
8. *Be kinder to yourself and allow yourself to make some mistakes and learn from them.*
9. *Don't take your life so seriously. You still have time to be an adult.*
10. *You don't need to follow society's rules and obligations. Be yourself and do what you want.*

I love you, Aga, and I'm so proud of you. I'm pleased you're growing, following your dreams, making plans, and changing them. The way you and your body look makes me feel so amazing right now. I envy you that body. Take care and love yourself.

Your older YOU

How did the event change your life?
In the very early part of being a woman, this event pushed me to try to control my body and weight. I was always on a diet and trying to eat less, meaning that I controlled the amount of food I gave my body, even though this was completely unnecessary. I didn't learn how to like my body, but I learned how to control it, and it took me a lot of time and energy not to do it anymore. Seeing this experience from

a distance showed me how unhappy I was because I tried to please, but who and/or what exactly, I don't know. Definitely not me.

As a Skin Sensei, I see the same patterns: control of every single imperfection, pimple, or blackhead. It's so frustrating, and it's so tiring for everyone who does it.

As an adult, it came to me that I didn't want to be a prisoner of my twisted perceptions or trends imposed on me by the market. Only with hindsight did it show me how much grief and anger had been with me all these years concerning my body. And I didn't want to waste my life on it anymore. I finally decided to enjoy my body.

What lessons did you learn from this experience?
We want to feel beautiful in our bodies and in our skin. We do so many things to feel beautiful. Often it may look like we sacrifice ourselves to feel good in our skin, yet somehow, we still don't. The reason why is the unrealistic expectations created by the beauty industry and imposed upon us. We place our confidence in fake photos on Instagram, in paid recommendations by influencers, and on social media's fake reality.

But we are unique, every single one of us, and we shouldn't adapt to any beauty trends or canon. We shouldn't hide our imperfections as these imperfections on our skin or our overall appearances make us who we are. They make us unique and special and should give us strength instead of shame or fear of rejection.

What would you tell other people who might be experiencing this in their lives?
I could say to be strong, be confident, and don't fall prey to this fake beauty pressure, kind of a beauty pep talk. Still, I know from my experience how difficult it is when you fight with your skin and feel like you are failing all the time. You lose hope that it will get better. So instead, I would say, 'I feel you. I'll be with you whenever you need me. I feel your anger and frustration, and I feel your desperate search for the right solution. I'm here to give you hope. Let the tears drop on this page and release any emotion. I'm here to enable you to stop fighting with your skin. She still might be your best friend.'

What are some of the things you would have changed about the situation if you could have?
Throughout my life, I have learned that nothing happens without reason. Life events that seem unpleasant, frustrating, and unnecessary have always led to positive endgames in my life. I learned to trust in my life, and that's why I wouldn't change anything because if I did, I wouldn't be where I am. I believe I was supposed to feel it, live with it, get to the point of writing this story, and find the missing dots in my life.

If this experience, from my teenage years, was somehow the reason I ended up educating people about skin, skincare, and how the beauty industry tries to manipulate us, I'm glad I went through all of this. We say that story matters, so I let this story matter and help others feel better about themselves. I'm more than happy to share it.

Any final words?

We let other people dictate how we should look and how we should feel in our bodies and our skin. The truth is that we will not accept ourselves unless we get to know who we are, what we feel, who we want to be, and how we want to be seen. It is our job to decide if we wish to follow the unattainable beauty trends or if we genuinely feel like ourselves. Unfortunately, we can still observe that instead of being an aspiration for many wonderful people, beauty trends make us hostages to their requirements.

Don't let them do it anymore. It's time to empower our beauty on our own.

How can people get in touch with you and see the work you do?
Podcast: Beauty and the Beast: www.skinsensei.io/podcasts

My Sliding Doors Moment

Clair Carrington

Energy Alignment Coach creating a safe space for spiritual women over 35 reconnect with their soul's purpose, to rediscover what lights them up and to fulfil their dreams.

What are you passionate about and how are you contributing to the world?

I know that deep inside every woman is a strength she can call on at every opportunity, a strength that can support her through life's obstacles and give her the freedom she deserves in life. It's my mission to guide women to find that internal strength through understanding their own energy and knowing that they create their own reality by discovering their own true purpose.

Describe a pivotal moment in your life that you would like to share.
Is it strange to say that I can't remember much about the first nine years of my life? I've searched my memory bank, and all I can find are what I would consider to be 'normal' childhood experiences, ones that perhaps give away my age, like coming in from playing with friends when the streetlights come on and the BBC test card being shown when no programmes were being aired!

Family was a huge part of my life on both my mum's and my dad's side. My weekends were filled with cousins, aunties, uncles, and so much love.

I spent my seventh birthday in France, my first holiday abroad, perhaps cementing my love of languages and other cultures.

Both of my parents worked, and from what I could tell, they were happy. I don't really remember any arguments happening, not until what I'm about to share with you.

The word blissful keeps coming to my mind when I think about those early years.

So to be taken not long before my tenth birthday from the normality of my life with family, friends, and the home I loved so much into a whirlwind of confusion, anger, violence and control was incomprehensible to me. My mum had had an affair, and it tore my parents' marriage apart. It devastated my dad, and even at my young age, I could see and feel his heart break.

Trying to tell the truth to both parents about your feelings and not wanting to make the situation harder for them is tricky, and yet it was a skill I mastered. As an adult, I can see that I was trying hard to make them both happy. It was easier than having to deal with the emotions I was keeping at bay. I just wanted to know that they loved me.

Alongside living with all of this, I had to make new friends at a new school in a new town.

The need to feel loved, liked, and fit in played a big part in shaping my personality over the next few years. In fact, this whole experience did.

Looking back, what made it such an important part of your journey? It will take me many years of reflection and working through my thoughts, beliefs, and emotions about what happened during the three short years of living with my mum and her husband and the subsequent confusion through my teens and twenties.

Those years formed a core belief inside of me that no one on this planet deserves to be treated with so much disrespect, violence, and utter control from another person. I now recognise that those who stay in such situations aren't weak — they are scared. They feel worthless and often feel as though there is no way out. These women — and in some circumstances, men — live with narcissistic bullies.

I wish with all my heart that I knew then what I know now. I wish I could empower my mum with the knowledge that might have freed her from a miserable life.

Upon reflection, living in a household filled with domestic violence has given me the gift of knowing what I am worth and that I won't settle for less.

I have effortlessly refused to be made to feel small. From my early teens, I have always known that I would be independent, forge my way through anything and everything with which the universe presented me, and create my own path in life.

Becoming an Energy Alignment Mentor has allowed me to release all of the negativity surrounding my experience. It has freed me to reconnect with my mum and has made changing the lives of other women in similar circumstances a part of my purpose.

The confused little girl about which you are about to read has taken this experience and turned it around into a life so positive. I can empathise, through my own understanding, with women who have experienced domestic violence. I can guide them, lift them, support them through life's adversities, and most importantly, give them the tools to create a life that they will love.

Based on the wealth of knowledge, wisdom and experience you have now, what would you have liked to say to yourself back then?

I see you, Clair.

I see how amazing life has been up until now, with nine years spent surrounded by a family who loves you, having fun with your friends, and enjoying life.

I'm so sorry I have to tell you this, but within the next couple of days, your life is going to be flipped upside down, and nothing will feel normal again. You are about to experience, see, and hear things that no child should have to. You will bear burdens and carry secrets with you for far too long, feeling embarrassed by situations you had no choice to be in.

You will want to protect others so they aren't hurt, and you'll want to save those closest to you from living a life that is miserable. The hardest lesson in all of this is that you can't — no one can — save those who don't want to be saved.

The first confusion happens the day you are ripped out of school by your mum without goodbyes or explanations. We were leaving Dad, and he had no idea. You will know inside how much he is hurting, and it will hurt you inside, knowing there is no way you can help him. Your dad is your hero, and he doesn't deserve that amount of pain.

We move in with your grandparents. There are a lot of secretive conversations behind doors that you shouldn't be listening to, but you can by sitting on the stairs or turning down the TV, and you will make out that they don't agree with the decision Mum has made.

There will be times when she has 'dates' with her boyfriend when you are made to sit in the car for an hour or more so they can go for a 'walk in the fields'. Ask them if you can join them, test them, and see what they say! You won't be allowed, so instead, you are forced to sit in the car on a country road with Queen and Elvis Presley CDs to listen to, knowing they are having sex nearby. You aren't stupid, and there will be a time when you get out of the car to see them. You shout that you are bored to distract them, but it makes no difference. You really want to run away and get out of the car, but you have no idea where you are or where you will go, and the man in the tractor scares you, so you get back into the car.

You live with the hope that Mum and Dad will get back together, especially with Nana and Granddad and your uncles telling Mum to make the right decision. You just want to be back home, but she doesn't, not now that you are moving in with her boyfriend in a town where you know nobody.

You know from the moment you meet him that you don't like him. You can feel he just isn't a nice man. You don't know the word manipulative at your age, but that's the energy you pick up on.

You won't see your dad for a year now, and that will be really painful. It's hard to understand why your mum allows her boyfriend to make decisions in your life. What's it got to do with him? He's clearly making you feel like you shouldn't be around.

From the moment you move in with him, everything changes. It's such a volatile household, and I'm so sorry that you are going to experience this. Please know that everything you are about to go through will make you the person you are today.

One thing you will learn from living in a home controlled by an abusive man is that you will be able to sense the energy of how the day will be before you've even left your bedroom before they *have even woken up. I want you to learn to trust this feeling, this intuition; you will learn to rely on it more as you get older.*

It's a hard thing to watch, seeing your mum become a shadow of her former self, scared to drive to work and back in case the mileage on the car is wrong, fearful that a bit of fat might be left on the meat at teatime because the plate will hit the ceiling, and the fighting will begin, and you will absolutely dread the nights when they go to the pub, scared to be left in the house alone, knowing that when they return, it will only end in one way: knives, fists, screams, punches, and the phone being ripped out of the wall. You will hear violent sexual acts, and yet your once happy, bubbly Mum succumbs and allows this abuse to happen to her.

You won't know this right now. You will just know that these are all demonstrative behaviours of a narcissistic, controlling man who can't control himself so he tries to control others.

You will try to save Mum in the way any 10- or 11-year-old can, by running up the street and phoning the police or knocking on the neighbours' doors to help. Cuddling her in your bed behind the barricaded bedroom door, you will beg for her to leave, and perhaps neither you nor I will ever understand why she stayed. You will feel powerless.

It's in these moments that you make a vow to yourself that life shouldn't be that way. You promise that you will never let a man treat you in that way and that life shouldn't be that hard.

I'm sorry to say that it's no wonder you will want to spend every waking moment wanting to be out of the house. Due to your need to feel liked and wanted, you will hang out with the wrong crowd, drink, smoke, skip school, and shoplift. For the most part, you get away with it because at home, you are quiet, watching and waiting for the next argument.

That is until you are caught red-handed and taken to the police station. Trust me when I say that is the universe stepping in and changing the path you are on. That was your 'sliding doors' moment.

Within days of being caught and branded the ring leader of your group of shoplifting friends, you won't be wanted in the house. You won't know it at the time, but this small act will be your ticket to freedom and back to the stability and security you have craved over the last few years.

You will make that life-changing phone call to Dad to ask if you can move back in with him and move back to your reality. Between your spending time in the police cell and moving back in with Dad, the 'bastard', as you now refer to him in your head, will walk into your bedroom naked, swinging his dick around, and ask if you know what one is. Thankfully, Mum will be there to drag him away. Thankfully, you will move out a few days later. Your intuition tells you that this wouldn't be the last time he'd have done that if you'd stayed in that house.

Let's make no mistake—the years spent in such a violent household will change you, and you still feel the need to protect yourself and your mum, and so you hold the secrets of that house inside you. You won't tell Dad why, all of a sudden, it's okay for you to suddenly move back in with him. You feel a shame that you can't describe, so ashamed that you can't tell anyone about the abuse you have witnessed.

It feels like a big secret and something that happens behind closed doors. If the police and the neighbours won't acknowledge it's happening, then perhaps you shouldn't be talking about it to people, and you most certainly won't talk to friends about it. They all have normal lives, after all, and you want them to like you for who you are, not to pity you for what's happening at home.

And whilst the environment you are in now is so much better than before, you will still learn to craft your 'truth' to keep people happy.

Mum will encourage you to catch buses to make the two-hour journey to see her because she isn't allowed to come and see you. You will tell Dad that she's meeting you. Coming home in the dark on a bus is scary when you're only 13. Again, you bend the truth to fit the narrative because you know it's wrong, and you are trying to please both parents, who you love so much.

You long to feel loved. Those three short years of living with them felt like the longest, loneliest times. You miss your family so much.

Here is where you think it will get better, but I'm so sorry to say that the confusion reigns throughout your teens.

I wish I could tell you not to worry, but I know you will because it's unimaginable what life is like for Mum being with him alone now that you're not there. Somehow, she finds the strength to leave him, and each time he finds a way to take her back home. Seven times over the next five years, she will leave him, sometimes relying on family, sometimes going to a refuge. The last time she finds a flat in the village you live in.

She's finally safe, and you keep checking in on her regularly. The relief will be tangible, that is, until two days before your 18th birthday, when she disappears. Her flat is stripped bare. Your grandparents and uncles, her three brothers, are devastated. And just like that, you are abandoned. She's chosen him over you. At least, that's how it feels. In Mum's mind, she probably feels as though she's saved you from having to be around that kind of person. For you, it feels as though she's given up on you and her freedom.

The rollercoaster of emotions you go through is monumental. The hope you feel that she will start a new life away from him, free from the violence, and then the utter sadness and despair when she returns back to him. This time, at the age of 18, you decide that this emotional rollercoaster is taking its toll on your mental health, and you aren't going to try to find her. You have a life to live. You are a good student, and you have a future to look forward to.

I'm excited to tell you that you do just that. You go to university and spend a year in Madrid, followed by two years in Japan. All of this time, it will feel bizarre that she knows nothing about you, how much you have grown, and how independent you have become.

You pride yourself on making things happen for yourself, which is something you won't have seen your mum do. Each interview you go to, you are offered the position. You thrive on the masculine energy of getting stuff done, not realising that you are still in survival mode from the past. You seek out partners who need fixing and only realise later in life that it's because it's so much easier to fix someone else than it is to fix yourself.

Eleven years go by, and you start thinking about having a baby, and deep down inside, you know you can't start the next chapter of your life without closing the last one, so you reach out to Mum in the form of a letter, and the relationship will be rebuilt slowly. She's still with him, and you learn that it is not your job to protect her anymore, regardless of how painful it is for you.

It's not easy rebuilding a relationship with someone you believe abandoned you and whom you have gotten used to life without, and you know that you have your own healing journey to embark on, and this is when you discover The Energy Alignment Method. Know that becoming a mentor is the key to your own transformation.

Reading this, you may think that your life is going to be hard, difficult, and lacklustre; Clair, it's not. You have so much to look forward to, and so many other experiences that will solidify who you are. You meet a man who will prove that life doesn't need to be hard and that it's okay to lean into your feminine energy and allow him to look after you. You don't have to do it all alone. It will take some time to get used to. You won't feel worthy of a loving relationship that's easy, and at the same time, you know that you DO deserve this. Lean into it, darling, and allow yourself the happiness and security you crave so deeply.

As the years go by, you will find yourself drawn to campaigns that support women who are vulnerable, and you will even create a business that empowers women who are growing their own businesses to realise their dreams. You do this through energy work that allows them to release their limiting self-beliefs and build up their self-esteem — that's the 'yin' feminine side of the work you bring to them along with your own masculine, no BS attitude! — behind the scenes, with that systemising and getting-stuff-done zone of genius for which you are known.

I hope you can see that when I said that all of the experiences you are about to go through will make you the strong, independent, take-no-shit kind of woman you are today, it was the truth.

You had two paths that your life could have gone down, girl, and you chose the right one.

How did this event change your life?
This is a really tricky question. How would I know what life would be without experiencing this? This experience was the first trauma I can remember. There were more that I experienced later in life, and they have all brought with them an inner strength that I know I can call on when needed. Perhaps bizarrely, I only recently acknowledged that it was traumatic and was still sitting in my field of energy.

It didn't change my life; it simply created a different path than the one I thought I would take in life. There have been times in my life when I believed that the universe had it in for me. Big things in my life always seemed to end in pain and tears, many of them.

In my later years, all of this gave me the opportunity to grow and expand as I explored the hidden emotions that surrounded it.

What are some of the things you would change about the situation if you could?
I've always considered that we all have 'sliding door moments' in our lives; some are more obvious than others. I definitely experienced that when I was caught shoplifting. It was a time when one action changed the course of my life. Would I change anything about the whole experience? Yes. I wouldn't want my mum to be hurt and her freedom to be taken from her. All of that said, without this experience, I perhaps wouldn't have empathy for other children in similar situations or for women who find themselves in shelters, trying to escape violent relationships.

Any final words?

Sometimes, things have to go very wrong for them to go very right. I'm not sure who wrote that, but it resonates deeply with me, and I hope for you, too.

Please know that life will always present challenges and obstacles and that if you trust yourself, your intuition, and your energy, things will always work out in the end.

How can people get in touch with you and see the work you do?

https://linktr.ee/claircarrington

My Choice to Fight

Claire Gibbons

Health and Fitness Trainer. Passionate advocate guiding people to find their confidence and inner strength. Avid traveller, dog lover.

What are you passionate about and how are you contributing to the world?
Week after week, I see people almost afraid to step into a fitness class or the gym, feeling like they are being judged, watched, or even feeling like they can't do something. It's my mission to help those people on their fitness journey, to give them the confidence to step into that class for the first time, at whatever stage of their journey they may be. We all have the strength within us. We, as human beings, are capable of so many wonderful things if we could just tap into it. I have been extremely fortunate to have trained so many incredible human beings, and I continue to welcome more each day.

Describe a pivotal moment in your life you would like to share.
Imagine hearing the words, 'If we don't operate within hours, you may be paralysed.' I swear I felt my heart almost stop. My life

stopped for a moment. From then on, it changed forever. How do you even begin to comprehend those words?

I've had times in the past when things have happened to give me a bit of a wake-up call, never really believing that the universe was at play there, but oh, how wrong I was! Every single one of those past events was trying to give me the message to change my ways before things got worse. Well, they got worse. This time, it was completely different, I had no choice but to listen. I was dealt a real blow that shifted everything before I knew it. If only I'd listened a little earlier.

Following months—even years—of chiropractic treatment, I was still working every hour God sent, smoking at least ten a day and sometimes more, and drinking most weekends (when not working). My lifestyle was hectic, even chaotic at times. Little did I know that it was leading me down a path to my own detriment. You'd have thought I'd learn to slow down...

Like any other day at work, your back will be really giving you trouble, but that day, it feels different. Your legs feel weak and painful, and they let you down. In fact, they collapse from underneath you without warning while heading to the lift.

At that point, you remember a piece of advice from the chiropractor that will help you know what to do next: if the pain feels different, get yourself to A & E.

As I was being driven to A & E, I knew in my gut that something was wrong. It wasn't like any pain I had experienced before. My body trembled with pain. The only way I felt even a slight comfort was to lay across two chairs in the waiting room. Within a couple of hours, Mum arrived to be with me, and she noticed the trembling. A few hours later, I needed the toilet. It was at that moment I knew something was definitely wrong. I felt a numbness in my saddle region, and my legs no longer felt like my own.

As best I could, I went to the front desk to tell the nurses that things don't feel right at all. I explained the numbness I was feeling.

The nurses got me through pretty quickly, and they started numerous tests and questioned every aspect of what I was feeling, and in a lot of cases, not feeling. Before you know it, despite a pinprick test to the legs and saddle region, they discharge you with nothing but painkillers and an advice sheet on back pain. At that point, you are screaming in your head for someone to please listen to you, but the doctor's opinion surely had to be right.

Back home, my legs collapse again, only this time, I can't get up and am stuck on the floor for two hours or so, which feels like a lifetime. I shout at the top of my lungs for help, but it's the middle of the night, and everyone is asleep, so nobody comes. When I finally manage to get myself up, I go back to bed as quick as I can for some sort of comfort.

The next day, I ring my doctor for advice as the same thing happens as the day before. He advises a referral to the clinic for an MRI, but it will not be immediate. Again, I know this doesn't feel right, but I respect the doctor's opinion. Later that day, I lose control from the waist down, and fear grips me. I know the call to 999 is the most important one I will ever make.

When I arrive, the doctor administers morphine, and I feel my first bit of relief in over two days as my body finally begins to relax. As the night goes on, an MRI is carried out to find out what's happening, although in my head and heart, I secretly already know it is something serious.

Here come those words, the diagnosis I need to hear. The doctor reveals, after a long wait on the MRI table, that he has been speaking to the consultant on call at Cardiff Hospital for an emergency operation that night. I have a significant disc herniation that is crushing my spinal cord, and time really is of the essence.

'If we don't operate within hours, you may be paralysed.' Those are the first words I hear that make everything stop, just for a moment, and it is not a guaranteed outcome. The doctors can't say it will cure everything but that it is needed right now to even give me half a chance.

The operation is done and now begins the battle. It is the time to choose—should I let this beat me or fight it all the way?

Looking back, what made it such an important part of your life journey?
I was heading down a path of self-destruction, working myself into the ground to smoke, drink, and keep a house that was used as a hotel. That's how little time I spent there. I didn't see my friends much and didn't go out an awful lot, so my life was pretty much work, work, work.

The whole experience turned my life upside down with just a few words; I was completely shocked to my core. We always think things like this will never happen to us. I can't change what happened to me, but by raising awareness, I can help others to recognise the signs and listen to their instincts.

Looking back, the physical support is always what is concentrated on, but the mental health aspects are not at the forefront. This is a devastating, traumatic thing to happen to anybody that needs more support from the outset. Adapting to a spinal injury is something nobody should have to go through alone.

I was lucky to find fitness, which gave me a whole new lease on life physically, mentally, and spiritually. Fitness saved me from a dark place that nobody should have to go. This is why I now deliver fitness to the world, pushing hard past limitations to help others on their fitness journey. This has both physical and mental benefits. Sharing my story and what I do helps guide others through their own experiences, giving them hope that no matter how hard it gets, we fight for ourselves, and we become such powerful forces.

Based on the wealth of knowledge, wisdom and experience you have now, what would you have liked to say to yourself back then?

Dear Claire,

Here I am, writing back to you from the age of 36, now seven years down the line from where you are, the last year of your twenties. You and I both know that your twenties have not been kind to you at all in many ways, but this is going to top it all! You know as well as I do that you've been fighting an old back injury for a while with numerous hours of physio and chiropractic treatment every three months just to keep things at the same level. The funny thing is that you started running to give yourself a release from all of the rubbish you've experienced over the last few years, and that's how you hurt your back in the first place!

Now brace yourself because the time has come to tell you that after a fab weekend in London, things are about to go downhill fast. Prepare yourself for a rough ride, girl!

Today will seem like any other day at work. Your back will be really giving you some stick, but today it feels different. Your legs feel weak and painful, and they will let you down. In fact, they will collapse from underneath you without warning.

At this point, I want you to remember that one piece of advice that we got from the chiropractor that will help you realise what is going on. Remember how she told you that if it ever gets to the point where you lose control of your legs, they start to feel numb, you lose bladder and/or bowel control, or the pain gets worse, go to A & E; now is that time.

As you are being driven to A & E, even though you don't have all the symptoms, you will know in your gut that something is wrong. Please listen to that feeling. When you get to A & E, you will tremble with pain, so lie across two chairs. I promise you it will feel more comfortable (to a degree) and don't worry. Within a couple of hours, Mum will arrive to be with you. A few hours from now, you will feel the need to go to the toilet, and it's here that you know something is definitely wrong as you have started to develop numbness in your saddle region. Please listen to me now when I say you need to march as best as you can back to the front desk to say that you feel things are not right and explain what's happening. Mum also points out to you that you have stopped trembling — are you still in pain?

Needless to say, you now begin to worry, and the nurses will see you pretty quickly. After some testing and a lot of questions, even though you have numb legs and saddle region, you are going to be discharged with nothing but painkillers and an advice sheet on back pain, which, at that point, is almost an insult, but you trust the doctor's opinion, and off you go back home.

At home, your legs collapse again, only this time, you will be stuck on the floor for two hours or so, which I promise you will feel like a lifetime. You shout at the top of your lungs for help, but it's the middle of the night, and everyone is asleep!

The next day, I urge you to ring the doctor for advice as the same thing happens as the day before. You think, well, it can't be as bad as you think; you were just discharged yesterday — how wrong you are, my girl! Later, your body will completely let you down. From the waist down, you will lose complete control, and it must be said that fear will set in. You will know this is not right, and 999 needs that phone call, so don't hesitate to call them. Now, it's a race against time!

When you arrive at the hospital, you will be immediately catheterised. You won't realise it yet, but your bladder has retained over a litre of urine, a dangerously high amount! As the doctor administers the morphine, you experience the first bit of relief you have felt in the past two days. As you are rolled down for an MRI scan to finally find out what is going on, I think you and I both know, deep down, that the diagnosis you receive is going to throw your whole world upside down!

So, why, with the MRI done, are you still laid out on the table? What is going on for them to keep you there that long? It won't be long before the doctor reveals that he has been on the phone with Cardiff Hospital for an immediate referral. You have a significant disc herniation crushing your spinal cord and need emergency surgery tonight!

This time period with which you will be whisked off as quickly as possible offers vague memories due to the pain relief. The next thing you completely remember is waking up the next morning.

With the operation done and dusted, I want you to be aware that this will not be a cure-all. This is not the end of the journey. In fact, it is just the start, as you will be told that you have suffered a rare spinal cord injury called Cauda Equina Syndrome, which will leave you with permanent nerve damage to your legs, bladder, and bowel.

Every day from here will be an uphill struggle for you, but I can tell you this: you are more than prepared to deal with everything that comes your way, and you will face this head-on. You will find an inner strength you didn't even know was possible, rising out of the darkest depths to find yourself stronger than ever.

Remember when you were 13 years old and in school? You were easily led by strong characters and bullied on most days, either for being the 'ugly kid' or a 'total geek', and how it made you curl up inside your shell for a while, and most days felt hard. One day you'd had enough. For the first time in your life, you stood up to those popular kids, and that was where you started to learn to fight for yourself and take no bullshit. Take it from me, keep this quality, it will serve you well.

Or the time, at 16, when Dad pushed you to get a job literally straight out of school with no time to chill or no time to relax. At the time, you thought, **For crying out loud, he's being harsh. Give me a break, will you?** *But know this: it will instil a strong work ethic that will be your greatest weapon, and girl, you will need this and utilise it to the max.*

Fast forward a few years to 22. You and Dad don't get on very well at the moment for many reasons (no need for details here), but it will lead to a period where you don't speak to each other. A good few weeks will pass, but all will be well in the end.

Working hard has never been a problem for you, and that's just what you do to keep your house going, working all the hours you can, and focusing on trying to build your own life.

Finally, you feel as if life is going along nicely. You have two jobs, day and evening, a tidy little wage keeping you going, the house is coming together, and you're making it your own. You've also gotten back into a relationship with an ex (you came back together via some sort of twist of fate). It's been ten months already, and your heart feels so full, but something still doesn't feel right. Your partner has been acting a little strange for a couple of weeks, and you can't put your finger on why, but you think that his birthday is coming up, and he's not a great fan of birthdays; maybe that's it.

You get him a card and a great present and plan to surprise him on his birthday by turning up at his house to cheer him up a little. Approaching the house, you feel a wrench in your gut. Something feels off, but still, you can't figure out why. Prepare yourself, sweet girl, as this is going to hurt! You knock on the door, and a woman answers. You don't think anything of it as it seems he has a few guests, maybe some friends, visiting for his birthday, the same as you. He seems shocked and almost gutted to see you, so you feel hurt and decide to leave his gift and go home. You wrack your brain all night, wondering what's going on, so you ring him, and a woman answers. Suspicion sets in. You, being very stubborn and the whole don't-take-bullshit attitude you've inherited, question him and her. It turns out that he is leading a double life with you and her the whole time. Well, I can tell you that it feels like a huge kick in the gut and a knife through the heart all at the same time. Hurt doesn't even begin to describe what you are feeling right now, but girl, it's not over yet...

Six weeks later, you find out you are pregnant, and of course, the father is Mr Double Life. Shock, upset, love — all of these different feelings come to you, not knowing where to turn. You feel as if Mum will be so disappointed, and telling Mr Double Life is not an option at this point. You are still reeling from the breakup and trying to figure out your emotions. You are not even sure you want kids and especially not with him. He betrayed your trust and broke your heart in two, so you keep it quiet. Unfortunately, three weeks go by, and you lose the baby. Even though you were not sure you wanted children, your maternal instinct has already kicked in. Even in that short period of time, you know that you love the child already, so this is really hard for you to take. You feel so lost for some time, you grieve, you feel the loss, but it gets better.

These few events in your life I have told you about, this is why I know you will be okay with the news coming from the doctor. You are more than prepared for this. Yes, you will have a life-changing injury that will be the hardest thing you have ever had to deal with. It will feel like your whole world has come to a halt. You will grieve, you will feel the loss, your body will let you down, and you won't be able to control the situation. At 29, you will wonder why me? What did I do to deserve any of this? But you will get through it. You are already so strong from all of the events that have passed. This will be no different. You will rise up like the warrior that you are.

You will find it hard at first — hours of physio, hydrotherapy, gym sessions, the physical aspects you now must deal with, fighting the doctors to help you get self-catheterisation in place, and the nerve damage will leave so many long-term effects, and not just physically. Mentally, you won't feel yourself. You won't recognise who you are anymore. You always liked to be in control of your life, and this will be hard to stomach, but I can tell you one thing: do try that first group exercise class at your local gym. It will be the start of a new path for you, one you are destined to follow!

In the future, you will be a fitness trainer who inspires people, day in and day out. You didn't allow yourself to become a victim of your injury. Instead, you faced it head-on and said, 'No, I will find a better way.' You have surpassed all expectations and pushed so many limits, going out of your comfort zone daily to take fitness to the world, which was what helped you through this horrendous trauma. You are giving so much joy back to society and helping others grow, be a better version of themselves, and find an inner strength they never thought possible.

You are following your dreams, and they are coming true in so many aspects. Girl, you have come through this so strong, and you should be so proud of the person you have become. You may not believe it at the time, but you will be grateful that all of this happened. You took the hand of cards you were dealt and made it the best it could be. In doing so, you have become such a kind-hearted and strong soul. Trust your journey. You will prevail. Be patient with yourself, be kind to yourself, but most of all, be proud of yourself!

How did this event change your life?
My whole world was turned upside down. I never imagined that, at 29 years old, I'd experience this life-altering injury and how it would affect me for many years to come. I never imagined I'd have to learn to adapt to a whole new way of life, and I did not realise how I took such little things for granted each day.

I was smoking every day and drinking most weekends (when not working), so I wasn't kind to my body at all. I truly believe this was my wake-up call to change my ways before I was in a much worse place. Looking back, it did me a favour, and that made me a much better person. It is my belief that none of us ever truly knows what hand of cards we are going to get, but it's how we choose to deal with them that matters.

What lessons did you learn from this experience?
I never really used to believe in a higher power, the universe, or anything like that at all, but this journey I've been on taught me that the universe guides us whether we know it or not. We are all walking the path we are destined to. Without this experience, I never would have known how strong I was mentally or how the human spirit continues to fight on with such resilience. We all have

fight in us, and I've really used my fight to find my passion and take it forward to the world.

What would you tell other people who might be experiencing this in their lives?
Be patient with yourself. It takes time for our body to adjust and heal but never give up on yourself. There will be times that you are tested to your limits. The physical aspects will take care of themselves; however, it will also be a mentally tough journey, so don't be afraid to seek help from a professional. It's a tough journey on your own. Lastly, we know ourselves better than anyone, so please trust that feeling in your gut always!

What are some things you would have changed about that situation if you could have?
They always say that hindsight is a wonderful thing, but in this case, it may not have changed the outcome. If I'd have asked for a second opinion on my symptoms that night, maybe even fought harder to get an MRI one day earlier, the aftereffects may have been less severe, but who is ever truly to know?

All I know now is that there's a reason things happen. It may not be fully revealed to you for quite some time — maybe even never — but I know that this path was meant for me, and without all of this, I would not be the person I am today. For that, I am grateful.

Any final words?

Life sends us traumas and agonies at times, but know that they only make us stronger than we thought possible. I was dealt a tough hand of cards, but I chose to make it a winning hand. I became a warrior for myself.

We all have a choice. I chose to find my fight — will you choose to fight, too?

How can people reach out to you?

*www.instagram.com/claire_gibbons_*

Lame Ducks

Esther Rowan Wells

CEO of International Business & Mindset Mentor

What are you passionate about and how are you contributing to the world?
I provide individuals who don't quite fit in or are slight misfits a chance to improve their financial security, physical health and life/work balance. I show these individuals how to create tools, techniques and habits to support a positive mental attitude to help grow a very specific kind of business. Providing a vehicle to create sustainable income for them and their loved ones now and for generations to come.

I provide our community of misfits a home in which they finally feel, not only welcomed, but have a sense of belonging where together they can support each other to create the lives, each dreams of.

Describe a pivotal moment in your life you would like to share.
I guess this all starts with the fact that I have worked with several mentors in various stages of my life and career. Two of these incredible mentors are Tasha Powell Chen and Diane Shiels

Bettencourt. I have been working with both of these lovely ladies for several years now. They do most of their mentoring through 'The Science Getting Rich Academy' through various levels, and I have worked my way to the elite.

Tasha and Diane invited the elites to a five-day retreat in Florida. As I lived in the UK, Florida seemed too far to go for just five days, so my husband and I turned it into a holiday. It was a perfect balance, time for the two of us in which we could do our own things and spend time with friends. It really was a very special holiday, and I tried very hard not to forget how great it was until 4th December 2021 changed everything.

Based on your wealth of knowledge, wisdom and experience you have now, what would you have liked to say to yourself back then?

Dear Est,

I'm sure you know this about yourself, and those of you who know me well will not be surprised to hear that I've done my chapter slightly differently than in my book, **Sisters and Brothers.**

A pivotal moment I want to talk to you about is something I'm currently going through, so I can't look back to give my younger self advice as it's happening right now, even as I write these words.

The last eight months have been truly life-changing. This eight-month period will cause you more physical pain than you will ever go through, but on the mental side, it will be so much easier than it could have been because of your past experiences and what you learnt from them that will give you grace, patience, and strength. So, let me take you back, and maybe then you will understand.

As I write this, you are currently a 44-year-old successful CEO of your own international business.

To help you understand, I am going to take you through six critical points in your life, the first one being when you were about 17. But before we start, I want to give you a massive hug, and I want you to know and to instil into every fibre of your being that you have always been and will ALWAYS be good enough.

I know that, up till now, you have found some things in your life pretty hard. You have been bullied most of your life, you have no self-esteem, your self-talk is hideous, you struggle with your weight, you have health issues, and your self-worth and self-love are almost non-existent.

I want to write about the girl who is just leaving the sixth form and about to go to the College of Care, as this college will change everything.

I know you won't believe how significant your time at this college will be, as it is only now, by looking back, that I finally understand, so how could you possibly know?

You discover a world filled with laughter, fun, love, and a sense of being 'home'. Not once in those few years of college did you question if you belonged; you were just a part of the group. For the first time in your life, you will make incredible close friendships with other girls that will smash the wall you have built around you to pieces. Although you try, this time, the wall fails to keep people out.

I wish I could build on this space and instil in you that you are an extraordinary person with such a massive heart, but you were never meant to fit in, and why would you want to? The most interesting individuals and experiences are just outside of the lines. As human beings, we are not meant to fit in a box.

You could save so much hurt if you only realised that the way you react to the world and the way you see it is completely unique to you. You must stop expecting others to react in the way you do, as all it does is lead you to feel hurt, disappointed, and let down once again. I know this will hurt you so deeply, and I am afraid to tell you that this will continue throughout your life. You will eventually learn the skills to look at the world through different lenses.

Maybe Mum was right when she called you a "lame duck". Maybe she could sense the unease in you.

You have always hated to see anyone unfairly treated, not given a chance to blossom into who they might be. Like a lame duck who has duckling misfits following you, you could always see the potential in people, the incredible swans they were meant to be. Maybe Mum saw something that you had not yet discovered. Maybe the reason she used to call you a lame duck was to encourage you to discover your purpose in this world, to stand out, lead, and 'do it your way' because you can inspire. Frustratingly, you easily see in others what you fail to believe about yourself. Not surprisingly, you will end up in a business that is all about helping other misfits just like you.

I wish I could make you believe this right now, but I know that I have a better chance of flying to the moon and back, as you always do things your way, including what you think.

Esther, it doesn't have to be this hard. You always choose the hardest route, and it will continue unless you learn that your thoughts and self-talk can and will affect your physical world.

The second critical event happens whilst you are still at college, although it is not directly related to your college experience.

Sorry to tell you, it's about then that Mum's health deteriorates to the point where you and Pod cannot continue looking after her without additional help. I'm not telling you anything you weren't aware of at the time, but what I do want to warn you is that, at this point, you really develop the habit of carrying a sense of responsibility for others.

This is the first time your mental strength influences your physical world.

This leads to the third critical point in our lives when we feel we have to choose whether to continue to care for Mum for the rest of her life or get on with a life of our own.

I want you to know that even though it feels like an impossible decision to make, you are a fantastic carer, but you are a crappy carer when it comes to your mum. You need to go get a life of your own and become Mum's daughter, and not her carer.

This is when you realise that if you get the right team of carers in place, you could go join Tegan in Oz.

Although it breaks your heart to leave Mum, this is the start of you discovering your own life and how to think for yourself. When you are away, you realise the amount of time you have spent with your Mum, how she has influenced the way you think, and how many things you actually have an opinion about.

You will have the most incredible experience in which you discover parts of yourself, and you will realise that you are actually quite a likeable person. You are fun, big-hearted, have a great sense of humour, and you are actually able to be independent. You are even pretty good at directions, especially because you can't actually get lost when you don't know where you are going!!

The fourth critical point in life is running away from a man who has just pinned you against a wall and tried to rape you.

Breathe and breathe again; you are safe.

When you've pulled yourself together, I want to tell you about the man who just tried to attack you. You will give him the nickname Harriet. He is someone whom you let into your life because you are so depressed and miserable that you don't realise the kind of guy he is. The problem is that Harriet is not a nice man. He represents everything you hate in human nature.

What I want you to take away from this horrible experience is that this wouldn't have happened if you weren't in such a bad place mentally.

In a strange way, Harriet did us a favour as he woke you up to the realisation of how down and dark you have been, and you make the unconscious decision to never let yourself get that down and dark again, leaving yourself open to such vulnerability.

Once again, mental thoughts create your physical environment. Please start to join the dots and realise that your mental health dictates your physical environment. I wish you would take this advice, but I'm not sure that you are really ready to hear it.

Critical point number five: over the next ten years of your life, you will work with different mentors, including Adam, Tasha, and Dianne, and read several self-help books. You will start to learn the importance of combining your mental health and your self-talk with the reality of your physical world. For health reasons, you lose over seven and a half stone, which, for someone who has struggled with their weight on and off for their whole life, is an important achievement.

There are three things that help you successfully reach the goal of this dramatic weight loss:

1. *exercise,*
2. *the products from your business, and*
3. *learning to change mental and physical habits.*

It's about this time that Adam will ask: 'What is it you hate most about your body?'

Your reply will be 'My stomach.'

Then he will say, 'Can you imagine living life without a stomach? You wouldn't eat, enjoy, or digest food in the same way.'

It affects so many parts of you, and life will never be the same.

From this point on, you start to understand all of the really ugly things self-talk used to say about your body. From then on, every time you find yourself critiquing a part of your body, you will check yourself. Just say how grateful you are for your whole body as the human body is an incredible thing three times to yourself.

The last critical period.

Over the years, you have had a rocky and argumentative relationship with Mum. At this time, you tend to only see the negatives.

Towards the end of her life, as she gets older and sicker and spends most of her time at home, in your opinion, she is just existing, just sitting in her wheelchair, getting more frightened of everything. I think she misses out on so much, which is sad.

We lose Mum in November 2020. Now, looking back on our relationship, I'm glad she wasn't here to watch and experience what you have been going through in these past eight months. Now, we can remember the positives and the good times, and for this, I will be eternally grateful.

In so many ways, you are our mum's daughter, and you will be determined to honour her by living your life with all of the great qualities we shared, our love of adventure, the way we see the world, and our desire to be creative.

As I write these words, I realise our mum was the first 'misfit' we experienced in life. She prided herself in doing things in the way she believed was right, not caring about what people thought, and living her unique life.

So, dearest Est and reader, I think it's time to tell you what happens to us on 4th December 2021 whilst in Florida. We slip, and our body goes one way whilst just the left leg goes the other, causing more damage than anyone would believe was possible. After five operations to try to save the leg, you eventually lose the battle, and they take the left leg above the knee. For the rest of your life, you will be an amputee.

I hope I have shown you through the critical points in this chapter and the power the mind has over our physical life. To put it simply, looking back on our life, when our thoughts were dark, bad things happened in our physical reality, but when our thoughts were positive and light, good things happened.

When you are in hospital, so many people will tell you how proud they are of how you deal with the accident. The point that I won't seem to make people understand is that it feels as if I have no choice. I wish I could make our loved ones see where I'm coming from, but we really don't have any options as to how we deal with this; this is the only way we know how. The frustration we feel and the lack of control we have is unexplainable, but it is still very raw, and I don't know how much to write now as it is our current reality. I don't want to mislead you into thinking we've never been frightened or scared; I just haven't let the feelings consume us. To be brutally honest, I am petrified about the next stage, which is to learn to walk again.

If I could change anything for us in this period of our life, I wish that it could have been less painful for all of those close to me, particularly our husband, Tim, and this is something for which I'm deeply sorry.

Looking back, what made it such an important part of your journey? Hindsight is a really lovely thing, but as I am still in the after effect of my accident, learning to walk, the emotions it created, the loss it created not just for me but for all of my loved ones, it's far too soon for me to look back and have any kind of hindsight.

How did these events change your life?
Without stating the obvious, I have lost half of my left leg, so in a split second, I went from being independent, freely able to go wherever I chose to go, to being dependent, spending my life in a wheelchair, and eventually using a metal leg.

But my accident is only a part of this story. The real message I want to leave you with is the power of your mind, and if nothing else, this has taught me how powerful it is, and I need to be careful how I use it. We all do.

What would you tell other people experiencing this?
Throughout my stay in hospital, everyone kept telling me how proud they were of me and how I dealt with my situation. Although everyone meant it from the most caring part of their heart, it felt like extra pressure, especially because I felt as if I had no choice.

For those of you going through something similar, you will feel as if you have to be responsible for everyone else's emotions, love, and grief for you. However, it's more important for you to just breathe and focus on your inner strength. You have to get YOU through. It is not your responsibility to protect or look after your loved ones.

My instincts, just like everyone else's, is 'You've got this. You can do this,' but I am not sure this is what you really need to hear. Trust your inner strength, and it will lead you through.

What are some of the things you would have changed about this situation if you could have?
The hurt it caused my loved ones.

Any final words?
Carpe Diem—Seize the Day.

How can people get in touch with you?
https://m.facebook.com/aloeholistics

Every Moment, Every Choice, Every Experience Made Me Who I Am Today

Kristi Maggio

Entrepreneur in Education, Author, Teen Mentor, and Inspirational Speaker

What are you passionate about and how are you contributing to the world?

I am dedicated to providing access to education and employment opportunities for youth around the world. For over 20 years, I have watched many children fail and feel inadequate merely because they didn't fit into the traditional education system. As a result, I started creating a system that addresses all students by providing what is lacking in the traditional model. Now upon graduation, these students can either receive meaningful employment in their area of specialization, go on to higher education, or even start their own businesses. For the first time ever, we can significantly reduce generational poverty because anyone can study and work from anywhere as long as they have a laptop and a signal.

Describe a pivotal time in your life that you wish to share.
We are defined by so many different moments in our lives that either lift us up or break us down. Two events occurred in my life at a very young age that I remember quite vividly. They both shaped how my life would play out. The first made me never want to ask for anything as it meant I couldn't provide it for myself. The second made me believe it was better to be seen than heard because you never know when someone will be at their breaking point the moment you need something.

After these events, I started stuffing my feelings down with food and vicariously living through my imagination. In the short time between the ages of seven and eight, I had become very overweight with little self-esteem. The idea of sharing my feelings or asking for help became foreign to me, and I didn't dare open my mouth for fear of being too needy, bothering someone, or being scolded.

Due to my weight, I was made fun of, often embarrassed and ashamed of how I looked. I became eccentric in my fashion to mask how I really felt so people would believe I was strong and confident. However, I was in constant turmoil and felt very alone. I chose to be rebellious and hang out with exactly the opposite group of people my dad wanted me to just to get his attention because he didn't come around much. My parents had separated and divorced by the time I was seven, and I didn't really have a great relationship with my dad in my younger years. Therefore, I stuffed down how I felt inside, spent most of my time in my room, and escaped into my imagination.

The truth is, I was always looking for something that would make me feel whole. I just wanted to be loved, to be pretty, to have my imaginary world be my reality. In my senior year, I decided to do a lifeguarding course. At that moment in time, I was 5'5" and 218 lbs. From my perspective, that was not exactly swimsuit material! The pre-test to be a part of the course was to swim down and back the length of the pool. Most students were on the swim team, and it took them 30 seconds. For me, it seemed like an eternity, a never-ending two laps, and I wanted to give up, but I didn't. Completing the test and not quitting became the fire I needed to believe in myself and realize I could do anything I set my mind to. This was a big turning point for me.

By the end of that year, I felt good and had lost weight, but the unfortunate part about just losing weight is that you do not address why you were overweight, to begin with, and that led to a constant rollercoaster in the 'battle of the bulge'. I used food to cope like an addict who uses drugs or alcohol. So, when the devastating event of having my heart broken for the first time happened, I decided I didn't need anyone or anything, and I circled back to food.

I couldn't cope at all, and I decided that if I couldn't control what others did, I could control what I did, and here is the power of what happens when I set my mind to doing something. I began restricting food but also bingeing in moments of weakness, and that shouldn't happen. I couldn't be weak; I needed to be strong! Anorexia started settling in, and when I realized I needed to eat but would overeat at times, so did bulimia.

I was 20 years old when this started. I had struggled with eating issues and depression all my life because I never addressed what was really happening on the inside and had used food as a coping mechanism for a very long time. Finally, at the age of 34, I went to an eating disorders clinic, and at 36, I realized that I was meant for so much more.

My mission today stems from all of this. Helping young people have a voice, and giving them the tools to be confident and not feel inadequate is what drives me to do what I do. I know how they feel when they don't seem to fit in anywhere, when adults sometimes aren't kind, or the world has not guided them in the right direction. It is my burning desire to show them that they are enough just as they are and that they can do anything they set their minds to.

Looking back, what made it such an important part of your life journey?
Had I known then what I know now, I would have had a very different experience. I would have understood that adults sometimes say and do things they don't mean, but that doesn't change the effect it has on a child. They don't realize the scar it can leave on the little person who is just learning to navigate through life. Often, adults act out toward children because they are frustrated with something in their lives and they take it out on them because they can. Everyone is going through something all the time, but it is our responses to what we go through that make a big difference to the people around us. Our responses can have lasting and detrimental effects or a positive impact on someone else's life, depending on how we react to a situation.

As a teen feeling insecure about myself, I never realized that other teens were just as self-conscious and uncertain about themselves as I was, all of them looking for the right place to fit in. There is so much pressure as a teenager to fit into the 'societal norm,' and it is carried with you as an adult if you don't do something about it. When I realized that I was likeable for who I was and stopped trying to please everyone around me, so much began to change. What I overcame, the circumstances I faced, and the good and bad choices I made have all led me to where I am today. These experiences have allowed me to relate to young people in a way that many cannot, and for those with whom I cannot relate, I wrote a book with stories of great people who overcame different adversities as children to be who they are today. So now, I have a tool I can use at any given time to help young people see that they can overcome the challenges life presents them as well.

I want children to be seen and heard, no matter who they are or where they come from. I want them to know they were not put on this earth to fit in but to stand out, just as the great quote by Dr. Seuss goes, 'Why fit in when you were born to stand out?' I want them to be comfortable asking for help and love what they do instead of feeling as if they just have to do something because they were told to.

You see, I am strong; I am courageous; I am confident; I am enough; I am unstoppable. It has taken me so long to believe this, to control my mind and not let the fear and doubt keep me from sabotaging myself and escaping back into an imaginary world. It has truly come to pass that I am creating what I imagine, and nothing can stop me but me. It is through the previous pivotal moments that I hid, too afraid to realize my true potential, feeling as though if I succeeded there would be nothing to work toward anymore. I would find excuses and make up lies to sabotage myself, so I could save face in case I didn't succeed.

If I knew then what I know now, things would have been very different, and I want to bring this knowledge to the younger generation to guide them into having the right mindset and learning what school doesn't teach but should.

Based on the wealth of knowledge, wisdom and experience you have now, what would you have liked to say to yourself back then?

Dear Kristi,

It has been a while since I've seen you; however, you have always been close to my heart, and I think of you often. I know you're upset, and sometimes you just don't understand why things are the way they are, but you don't need to worry because you are perfect just the way you are. However, I am writing this to you because there are some things I need to share with you that you should know early on. I wish I knew then what I know now, and I wish I had someone to do this for me.

Your experiences are ultimately going to define who you become, something that I know right now you don't understand. Do you recall the moment when you asked the neighbor to go for ice cream, and you got into trouble for asking? I know that you felt really bad because you were told never to ask for things from other people, and you didn't listen. However, as a young girl, you didn't really see the harm in asking to go for ice cream, but you were scolded because you were taught that it is rude to ask for things from other people; you should first wait to be offered or invited, and you were told to never ask again. That's really difficult for a five-year-old to understand. All you really knew is that they often invited you when they came for a visit, and you thought it would be a great suggestion as you could have really gone for ice cream at the time!

Soon after that, another event will take place when you are reprimanded once again for asking, and that just seals the deal in your mind that you are better to be seen than heard. I will not go into the details, but the person who did this didn't mean it. They were just surviving as well, but you internalized it. You will play small after this happens and be afraid to use your voice to fulfil any of your needs or wants.

Subconsciously, you will carry these events with you for a very long time. You will feel like you need to wait for permission to ask for anything, and when you do ask for something, it will feel wrong. Don't be afraid to ask for anything if you need it or want it. Understand that you deserve great things, and the worst thing anyone can ever say to you is 'no.' I give you permission, and you can take comfort in knowing that, no matter the outcome, at least you asked. You will miss many great opportunities because you don't allow others to help you simply because you won't ask.

You will start to stuff down your feelings and your emotions with food, and that will be your coping mechanism for many years to come. I'm here to tell you that it's all right to express your feelings; you don't have to keep them inside. They are valid, and you deserve to be heard. You see, sometimes adults don't understand the impact these moments have on children as they're growing up. They just do the best they can with what they know. I realize this doesn't help you now with what you are dealing with, but I hope it helps ease some of the pain and burden you carry.

Your dad will leave soon, but it's not your fault. He didn't leave because of you. You may not understand the reason he left or why adults sometimes can't get along, but know that he loves you even though there will be times when he does not say the nicest things to you. He has his reasons for doing what he does, even if they are hurtful. They are not your burdens to carry, and you do not need to spend your life trying to make him proud of you or make him love you. Eventually, when you are older, you will have a close relationship with him, and you will learn that the reason he wouldn't come around was not at all because of you. You don't have to feel guilty, unworthy, or unloved. You don't have to question whether or not you did anything that made him not want to be a part of your life — none of that was you!

You will be caught in the middle of arguments between your parents after they're divorced. You will, at times, even be asked to choose sides or feel guilty for choosing one way or another, and that should never have happened. You are not to blame. It is their inability to get along. Remember that you'll be caught in the middle, and you won't know what to do. Walk away, ignore them, or raise your voice and tell each of them how you feel when they put you in these situations. Just don't internalize it because it will eat away at you and consume you.

I know this is all difficult to grasp as you are still just a little girl, but I promise I will do my best to guide you along the way. Your identity and who you are will come into question a lot. Because you don't know who you are when you go through middle school and high school, you will have a difficult time recognizing who you want your friends to be. You will often move from friend group to friend group, but you never feel truly comfortable with one or the other because you are searching for acceptance in others and to belong to something, but really, it's not the other people who don't accept you; you don't accept yourself.

The choices you make are often questionable. One, in particular, is a very dangerous moment that could have changed your life in a very different direction. It was the moment when you chose to lie and go out with your friends as opposed to spending the night where you said you were going to be. At that moment, you will be carrying a knife with you. You'll be in a dangerous place, and you will come face to face with what could have been the end in a split second. Don't be afraid; you will be okay. You might wonder why I am telling you this. It's not to scare you, but I want you to make better choices as you grow up. Realize that there are consequences and look into what those consequences could possibly be before acting.

I think that's the problem with so much today. As adults, we often tell children not to do things without explaining why, and I'm telling you this so that you will be more cautious and not feel as though you need to put yourself at such risk to try to fit in. You weren't born to fit in; you were born to stand out!

Even though you will be burdened being overweight for the majority of your life and eventually battle anorexia and bulimia, there comes a day when you decide you have had enough, and you put yourself in the hospital. Finally, you begin to believe in yourself and not care about what others think. I want you to know that you are beautiful, and you don't need to feel ashamed or embarrassed. You don't need to look for something on the outside to make you feel good on the inside, and the day you realize this, you will truly be set free.

When you lose weight for the first time, you will start questioning people's motives for liking you. Having been treated in a certain way for so many years as an overweight person, you become skeptical as to whether or not people like you for you or because you aren't overweight anymore. I want you to know that what other people think about you is not important. What is important is how you feel about yourself. I want you to love yourself and never put a value on those who want to hurt you or put you down.

You will wander, searching for a place where you fit in, and for so long, you will feel lost, unwanted, and undesirable. There will then come a moment when you start to see yourself in a different light and have more confidence, when you start to challenge yourself and recognize a greater potential, but things happen to bring doubt into your mind. I want you to know that you are going to have great accomplishments in this life, bigger than you can ever imagine!

While what I have just told you may seem overwhelming, everything prepares you for your life's greatest work: helping youth believe in themselves, belong to something, and feel confident about who they are. You are going to dedicate your life to being a teacher, a leader, and a mentor. Eventually, you will open your own school in the Dominican Republic and start a foundation, for which you will sacrifice everything that everyone else wants from you so you can do what you love!

You are now on a mission to provide access to education and employment opportunities around the world. You will be the voice for children who have been born into situations that don't permit them to have a voice. You will help them stand out!

Remember that you are a sweet girl with such a big heart! You are always the first to help others; this is one of your best qualities. People do like you for you, so you don't have to question that. At times, there will be wolves in sheep's clothing, and people will take advantage of you. Be aware that most people seem kind, but not everybody is good.

As I look at you, I smile because you truly are a wonderful and brave little girl. I wish I could protect you from the world, but that will be your job to eventually take it upon yourself to guide and help other young people. You will try to protect them from the things that you didn't know. You are going to be an amazing grown woman, and all of the lessons you learn along the way, you carry them with you so you can help other young people learn from your mistakes and from your successes. You are going to change the world. You are going to help other children like you feel good about themselves, feel confident, and feel loved, so they don't ever have to go through what you did, or at least, whatever they are going through, you will help them through it.

You see, you have to experience all of the things you will go through because they are the learning experiences you will need to accomplish your mission in the world. Don't be afraid; there is nothing to fear. You will have strong faith. God will be by your side, and through those moments when you think you won't be able to make it anymore, He will carry you until you can stand on your own two feet again. Nothing you go through is meant to hurt you, but everything that happens is meant to bring you closer to your final destination. It's a happy thought, and you are strong enough to get through every struggle and find happiness in every pain.

Never look back unless it is to share a story about a lesson in your life you feel will help someone else. Do not dwell on the mistakes or the fear that you will make the same ones again; you are too wise for that. But there will be naysayers who will allow that doubt to creep into your mind, who will allow those errors, those moments of weakness to come trickling back in and make you feel like you will never accomplish what you are meant to; they are wrong! No one can stop your destiny except for you. Without pain, there is no purpose, and your purpose is a great one that people will remember for many years to come.

You will care when no one else cares. You will give when no one else gives. You will love when no one else loves... and for this, I couldn't be any prouder of who you are and who you will be.

So now, go outside and play! Run around and feel free. Don't be afraid to ask or burden anybody. You're just a little girl. Love yourself, and just remember that I will always be here for you!

Your dearest friend,

Kristi

How did this event change your life?
With all of the events that have blessed my life, I feel the most important one was completing the lifeguarding course. Swimming those two laps to qualify gave me a whole new inner strength that helped me believe in myself and build my confidence for the first time in 16 years. It was thanks to my aunt, who suggested it would be a great summer job that was in high demand and paid well over minimum wage. Those were the motivators! There needs to be something that ultimately pushes a person and motivates them to do something and follow through with it. Knowing I could make $16.00 an hour instead of $5.00 was the catalyst, the initial push. However, in the end, what I got in return was priceless, as it changed

the trajectory of my future. It gave me an entirely new outlook on life and what I could accomplish. At this moment, I understood that everything comes with challenges, but the challenges can be overcome if you persevere, push through, and never give up.

What lessons did you learn?
Feelings and emotions are valid. We all need to be able to express them in a healthy way. We must be willing to address the root of any challenges we face. If we don't, then it will be like trying to cover a deep wound with a bandage. To get to the root of anything, you must be willing to ask yourself questions about why you aren't achieving what you truly want in life. For the longest time, I was not willing to do this, and I played the part of the victim instead of the victor.

Another important lesson I learned is that adults must remember that young people don't understand what we are going through. They haven't had all of the experiences we have had, and they don't know how to navigate life the same way that we do. We must be careful with our words and help children understand why people say or do certain things. We must also realize that our system and society have set limiting beliefs on what we can do, and we must continue to allow ourselves and young people to believe we all have unlimited potential, that we are all different and unique, and we must appreciate each other for who we are, not who we think we should be.

What would you tell other people who might be experiencing this in their lives?
The mirror is your friend. That person you are looking at needs you to love them and believe in them. You are perfectly made, and if you don't love yourself, then no one else will. Realize that your true potential is well beyond what you think is possible. We are like icebergs, only able to see the tips of what we can do, but if we look down deep, there is a whole lot more left to discover. Express your feelings, don't hold them in as they will cause you pain and possibly make you sick. If someone doesn't like that you express how you feel, then they don't have to listen to you, but it is your choice to have a voice. You are not meant to play small, sit on the sidelines, or be invisible. You are the lead actor or actress in the movie called 'Your Life.' Play it well, take the lead, and never allow fear to hold you back from achieving what you want.

What are some of the things you would have changed about that situation if you could have?
Nothing. Every moment, every choice, and every experience made me who I am today. Even the setbacks have been setups for something greater. I truly believe I went through everything I did because they were the lessons I needed to learn to become who I was meant to be. My faith keeps me grounded, and I know I will get to my final destination. I may be 're-routed' a few times; however, there is a reason for everything. When a door closes, when a relationship ends, when someone betrays you when a loved one passes away, these are all heartaches, but someone once told me that we grow through what we go through, and so I needed everything to happen in my life just as it did.

Any final words?

I will leave the final words of others who have inspired me in my journey:

'And so I tell you, keep on asking, and you will receive what you ask for. Keep on seeking, and you will find. Keep on knocking, and the door will be opened to you. For everyone who asks, receives. Everyone who seeks finds. And to everyone who knocks, the door will be opened.' — Jesus Christ, Luke 11:9-10

'Whether you think you can or think you can't, either way, you are right!' — Henry Ford

'God, grant me the SERENITY to accept the things I cannot change, the COURAGE to change the things I can, and the WISDOM to know the difference.' — Reinhold Niebuhr

'Be a "YES, I CAN" person in a no I can't world!' — Bruce Pulver

'It's not hard work; it's HEART work. Nothing is ever hard when it comes from the heart!' — Kristi Maggio

How can people get in touch with you and see the work you do?
www.kristimaggio.com

Rescued from Her Suffocating Shell in Hell

Leigh Anne Gardiner
The Imperfect Disruptive Coach and Facilitator, OTR

What are you passionate about and how are you contributing to the world?
I have a passion for empowering women who are stuck in the destructive pattern of 'Shame and Blame.' They live in a world surrounded by toxicity and wear a multitude of masks that are false excuses to hide behind when inside they feel as if they're dying. They find themselves in the fetal position behind closed doors only to dry their eyes a moment later, put the 'I'm fine' mask back on so they can return to their lives and pretend, when deep down, they crave the freedom to be raw and real with their truths, and live in pure authenticity, being perfectly imperfect as they are.

Describe a pivotal moment in your life you would like to share.
I want to take you back to the most pivotal time in my life, a time when every ounce of strength I had was tested, mentally, emotionally, spiritually, and physically. Looking back, that 'time and

test' proved that I would never be the same again, and I can say with 100% certainty that I haven't been the same since that night.

Then again, there's no way for me to know who I would have become if not for the unseen, unexpected domino of devastating events.

(Christmas music playing throughout the house)

On Christmas Day, 2004, my family and I went to Mom and Dad's to celebrate like we did every year. Holidays with family were Mom's favorite time of year. MawMaw, Grandpa and the whole family were all together, and the sounds of laughter and pure innocence came from Mom's six grandkids as they played "dress-up' and whatever else their imaginations could conjure up.

We listened to Mom and Dad playing Christmas carols, Mom on the piano and Dad on his guitar. It was a family tradition. This was the *last* family tradition.

Something was off that day. It was my mom. She had a silk scarf around her neck, tied as if she were hiding something. I looked closer and couldn't miss the suspicious 'lump' underneath. (My intuition spiked.)

I had seen so much, too much when I worked in the Acute Care/ICU, and I felt sick to my stomach. A sense of urgency rattled my nerves. She needed to see a doctor, ASAP. It had been 37 years since she'd seen a doctor, and that was only because she was giving birth to her only daughter: me! (Ugh!)

Regardless of my efforts, she refused to go to the doctor's until every single Christmas decoration had been taken down first.

Finally, on January 4, 2005, I took her to see an ENT. Then I heard it, my biggest fear: 'You have Stage 4 Parotid Gland Cancer,' the doctor said after her needle biopsy. 'It's aggressive.'

She was immediately sent to MD Anderson Cancer Center where her life changed. Forever. And so did I.

I felt lost and I feared loss.

After Mom's cancer diagnosis in January 2005, the journey of her intense treatments of weekly chemotherapy and daily radiation began. Dad and I traded off taking her to her treatments. I took the night shifts. I went to every doctor's appointment. I shaved her head and went with her to shop for wigs. It was intense, but the Hope and Faith I carried inside gave me the strength to do the impossible.

Eventually, the treatments finally took their toll. She was too weak to walk more than three feet at a time. The doctors stopped all treatments immediately. Her five-and-a-half-foot, 92-pound frame weakening rapidly. The tumor grew at warp speed. It eventually affected the nerves in her face and left her paralyzed as a result. She slurred her words when she spoke, and the cancer spread to her brain. She began to hallucinate.

In 2007, I was a single mom (divorced in 2006 after ten years of marriage) with two beautiful children. I had a seven-year-old son and a five-year-old baby girl. They would end up being my saving grace and the reason I made the decision to rise from my own ashes of despair later that year.

Barely.

It was the night before the first day of school, my daughter's very first day of kindergarten.

There we were, my brother Greg, Dad, the hospice nurse, Mom, and myself. She was lying in a hospital bed that had been set up in their bedroom. She was in a coma.

The hours passed slowly and quickly at the same time. We knew she was going to die; we just didn't know when.

My brother and I sat outside her room. Waiting.

I'll never forget what came next.

The hospice nurse opened her bedroom door and said, 'She's going. It's time.' He motioned for us to come in. My brother and I were on either side of her, holding her hands. That's when the completely unexpected happened.

Mom woke up from her coma.

Looking back, what made it such an important part of your journey?
Looking back at my life it has been a painful yet healing process at the same time. I used to wonder why we seem to learn a lesson or see parts of our lives with so much clarity in 'hindsight.' Why not in the moment? Wouldn't that prevent so much pain?

I quickly learned that the world doesn't work that way.

We have to go 'through it' and come out on the other side to finally be able to breathe, see the light piercing through the heavy darkness we've felt, and then finally, we see the lesson we were meant to learn all along.

I was forced to grow up, face my own truths, my insecurities, and overcome challenges, 'or not,' as we all are. I just happened to be forced by sudden, expected, unexpected, gut-wrenching, soul-piercing pain.

Pain was the weapon or instrument used, front and center in my life.

...and in my heart.

Facing adversity head-on became a regular occurrence in my life. Sometimes, I jumped over the hurdles, while other times, I crawled and bawled just to get to the other side, always fighting to get back to who I was always meant to be.

'Sunshine,' always sees the glass half full and rises above what tries to hold all of us down.

As the story continued to unfold, I learned that dealing with my emotions, talking about the loss, emptiness, and haunting fear, is almost as important as the air we breathe. I didn't acknowledge my pain or even give myself permission to feel whatever the hell I needed to feel in those moments.

Without judgment.

Instead of putting on a much-needed oxygen mask, I mastered the energy-sucking skill of putting on fake masks (plural).

They were the masks I wore as a shield in the hope of hiding my truth.

Some of the masks I wore were 'I'm fine,' 'Good, thank you, how are you?' and 'Nothing's wrong.'

That was furthest from the truth, and with every word I forced, every tear I stuffed down, every knot in my throat I swallowed and rejected, I continued to tell myself a destructive, self-inflicted, made-up, bullshit story that as long as I could carry the enormous burden without falling apart, I really was 'fine' and 'okay.'

In actual reality, it was one big, gigantic, false narrative that resulted in a level of pain I couldn't and can't articulate.

I became an expert at 'self-sabotage.'

I didn't feel like I was allowed to be happy. Somehow, I had made up my mind that if I laughed, smiled, or even allowed the tiny light still inside of me to be seen, it would mean I 'didn't care' about the events that ultimately led me to the empty, cold, dark place I would eventually find myself.

So instead, I walked through each day feeling as if someone was sucking the life out of me.

Meanwhile, 'I'm F.I.N.E.'

Oh, I was 'F.I.N.E.,' all right.

'I'm F.I.N.E.' meant 'I'm Fucked up, Insecure, Neurotic, and Emotional.'

I would try to look put together for the day (showered, makeup on) as I struggled to find the strength to 'appear' and 'sound' F.I.N.E., while maintaining some semblance of composure.

My eyes were often swollen from crying behind closed doors.

I would find myself collapsing wherever I was.

Standing, sitting, or existing.

As soon as I was safe from the world's questions, adulting, being a single mom, and feeling odd stares everywhere I went, I lost it.

I felt as if there was a volcano inside of me threatening to erupt.

Then, when I was all alone, it erupted. Not for long, though. I would put my mask back on and will the hot lava to stop.

Until the next time.

Somehow, I believed I was protecting those I was close to from seeing what I went through emotionally and physically, as the grief, loneliness, and depression became all-consuming and settled within every fiber of my being.

Destruction, devastation, despair, and depression felt like the slow death of my soul.

So, I fought for my life as well as the strength from within to push through each hour. I succeeded for quite a while, and ironically, being able to stay strong ended up being the fuel that fed the self-imposed *pressure to remain strong and never, ever break.*

No. Matter. What.

My two precious children were too young to understand that kind of sadness. I wanted to shelter them from ever feeling what I was feeling.

Deep down, I knew I couldn't risk even the smallest crack in my 'composure.'

If I got too close to the edge, my entire being would come crashing down.

I got too close.

Four years of 'holding it together,' 'being F.I.N.E.,' and moving forward in life was the beginning of the end. My entire being would come crashing down almost overnight. I remember what it felt like as my determination to 'stay strong' weakened, and I literally felt the layers of who I had become start peeling away and hitting the ground. Each layer sounded like shattered glass.

Now I see that my strength and resiliency were born out of complete devastation, bound to hold a million fragile pieces of pain together that I would carry around inside, disguised with a mask. Hence, shattered glass with a million sharp pieces left behind in the destruction, each of them broken in a different direction.

'Careful where you step, Leigh—there's broken glass all around.'

Looking back with a new 'pair of glasses,' it's crystal clear that my fall was the result of my relentless will to stay strong, which began to feed my own pattern of denial. I was in survival mode—fight or flight. That would become my 'normal state' for the next 15-plus years. It was a place I would live, filled with the denial of the invisible scars I hadn't dealt with from my divorce in 2006, and then the galaxy of scars where illness and disease lingered from the scars that were formed in 2007.

Based on the wealth of knowledge, wisdom and experience you have now, what would you have liked to say to yourself back then?

Leigh Anne, your pain and trauma matter. You matter. You are enough. More than enough. You're not weak if you share your truth, pain, and loneliness, but if you try to hold it inside, it will destroy you from the inside out until...

Allow yourself to be vulnerable, and if you fall, you'll fall into the arms of the many people who love and support you. I admire your unwavering determination to be independent, but Leigh Anne, sometimes being too 'independent' can lead to isolation which is a death sentence for your spirit and soul. You're meant to radiate Sunshine. You're meant to dance. You're meant for something indescribable in this lifetime, and someone needs to hear your story. Don't leave this earth with a single regret.

...oh, one more thing, Leigh Anne: never minimize the precious, unique, vibrant, magnetic woman you are.

Now, go out and own your uniqueness!

I wasn't in denial; I was denying myself the right to grieve.

Big difference.

My Leigh Anne,

I'm writing to you in the hope that you'll trust my words and follow my guidance. Angel, Mom is about to wake up from her coma and share her innermost wisdom that will be the beginning and ending of your life as you know it. The cancer has spread to her brain. The hospice nurse will be there 24/7. You're going to refuse to leave her side, but she is withering away, Leigh, and her body is beginning to shut down. Her tiny, 92-pound, five-foot body is less than 60 pounds, now, Leigh.

She doesn't look like Mom. Although you shaved her head on her birthday (4/13/2005) when she was losing all of her hair from the chemo treatment, these last memories will be photographs you'll file in your memory bank that'll haunt you in your future nightmares.

Leigh, I know you want to be by her side every minute and for every breath, but I want to warn you about the images and scenes you'll witness. They'll come back to you as flashbacks in your nightmares. Protect your eyes as much as you can. It's vital, and it has been vital for you to take care of yourself during these dark months and years so you can be there for her, your dad, and most importantly, your kids.

Speaking of Dylan and Leigh, it happens to also be the night (or morning hours, actually) before Leigh's first day of kindergarten and Dylan's first day as 'big brother in school' (he's now a third-grader).

Back to that night. You'll be surrounded by medical paraphernalia, forgotten wigs, and prescription bottles, all things that will forever represent 'cancer and death' to you. There is no longer hope.

The things you'll witness will be memories that stay with you for a lifetime, Leigh. Just focus on the next second, then the next, and breathe. One day, this will be the struggle you rise up from so you can Pay It Forward to whomever God chooses to place in your path.

You'll have done everything you could to preserve her dignity as you've watched the cancer grow from a golf-ball-sized tumor on her neck to complete paralysis on the left side of her face.

You and Greg will be in the family room right outside her bedroom door while the hospice nurse will be in her room, monitoring her vital signs. Dad will be in the backyard, away from the inevitable.

She will still be far away in a coma, Leigh, unable to communicate with you.

You'll have your brother with you, Leigh. Cherish that time, as morbid as it might seem.

You are strong, but no one is immune to trauma.

You will never forget what comes next.

You'll see her bedroom door open quickly, and you'll see the hospice nurse motioning for you and Greg to come in.

'She's going. It's time,' he'll say with certainty.

You and Greg will be on either side of her, each of you holding one of her hands in yours.

Then, the unexpected will happen.

Mom will wake up from her coma.

You'll hear Greg say, 'It's okay, Mom. We're here'.

Breathe. God has you.

She'll open her eyes and turn them to you, Leigh.

You'll be on the brink of hearing the most profound words of wisdom that will be a gift from God, whispered by the woman who brought you into this world, Leigh.

So listen closely.

'Leigh Anne, promise me one thing,' your mom will whisper just minutes before she takes her last breath. You won't notice that she's no longer slurring her words.

'Anything, Mom. What is it?' you'll reply.

'Promise me you'll stop putting everyone else first in your life. I'm worried about you. You have to take care of yourself.' She will get weaker, and her whispers to you will become softer as she begins to leave her physical body. Forever.

'I promise, Mom. I promise.'

As you lean over her hospital bed, you hang onto her tiny, frail hand with desperation, praying that moment never ends. It will be just the three of you. Until...it's just the two of you.

Your dad won't be able to come into the room. He'll know that he can't watch her die. He's already said **goodbye** in his own way. You've both been watching a slow death, not only from the cancer, but from the toxic side effects of chemo, radiation, experimental drugs, and everything in between that she has endured.

She'll barely whisper, 'I love you.'

You'll reply, 'I love you.'

'I love you,' she'll manage to say again through a shallow breath.

'I love you, Mom.'

Your body will experience the most intense and horrific sense of anticipation that has been one of your biggest, yet inevitable fears *in life: your mom passing away. It's a dark, heavy, suffocating feeling you've never experienced, but your intuition will know she's almost gone.*

'I love you,' she'll faintly whisper.

This time will be different.

It will be the last time you ever hear those words from her mouth while you're still here on this earth.

She'll never take another breath after that, Leigh.

While you stare at her chest waiting for it to rise again, you go into shock and feel a sense of emptiness you didn't know existed.

There will be a sense of finality at that moment because you'll realize there's no turning back. Your mom will pass on to heaven and forever be your angel. She won't be in pain anymore, but you will be, Leigh.

You'll feel an enormous and indescribable sense of loneliness.

You'll find yourself clinging to her body, which is just a shell while waiting for the morgue to come and take her.

The very woman who encouraged you to be perfect in every way.

For her, but to your detriment.

Especially where your physical appearance, the number on the scale, and the size of your clothes are concerned. You'll continue to carry that unobtainable expectation throughout your life unless you stop and remember the exact words she whispered before she died.

You could take care of yourself and stop putting everyone else first INSTEAD of trying to be what you aren't and won't ever be: perfect. Perfect doesn't exist.

The letter 'P' in Perfect = Pain.

Strive to carry out your Promise 'P' instead.

Mom's words carried more meaning than you realize. She was also saying to no longer worry about what other people think of you. This is the wisest statement she's ever said to you, advice that will be crucial for you to understand now, not later.

If you breeze over this request, you'll find yourself living a life of conflict, rebellion, emotional pain, and loneliness, consumed by guilt *and carrying a heavy, heavy burden full of the masks you'll begin wearing.*

You have a choice now.

Fulfil your promise and live a life with pure authenticity, peace, self-worth, and confidence, showing up in your own life as an *example of what it looks like to fully embrace all of your flaws, to be of service to others with **all of you.***

Maskless.

It's okay to feel lost, Leigh. You've lived every day for 37 years with a mom on this earth. You need to feel your feelings and not go through life pretending that you're 'okay' because let's be real here, Leigh, you're not 'okay,' and that's exactly where you're supposed to be now.

Actually, you're in fucking pain! Pain that's all-consuming...

If you grieve now, you can avoid the destructive events that unfold down the road in 2011.

Warning.

Open your heart, be vulnerable, and speak your truth. You're already loved and will be admired and respected by so many more down the road. Trust me. God has you.

The mask of 'I'm fine' is way too heavy for you to put on. Feel what you need to feel and allow yourself this gift, or trust me, hell will break loose for you, and this is your opportunity to avoid that.

It's part of living up to your mom's last wish.

Listen to me closely: you have been given a gift that you won't understand or recognize yet. You haven't woken up in life and discovered your true potential yet, and now you don't know who the hell you are.

You have a rare and indescribable level of strength inside of you that will carry you through the following days, months, and years of your life.

Sooner, much, much sooner, your gift of strength will be tested more than you could ever fathom in your lifetime.

Hang on, baby girl, *because the foundation of who you thought you were for 37 years will be ripped out from under you in a matter of seconds with zero warning.*

This time.

You'll need your gift more than ever in order to face the devastation of what comes next.

Nine weeks and two days later, you'll be putting dishes away while the kids are at the table, doing their homework. You'll only have been home from picking up the kids from school for about 30 minutes when you get the call.

The call.

'Leigh, you need to get the kids somewhere,' says your ex-husband on the other end of the line.

'What do you mean?' you reply, only to hear his voice quivering with a sense of urgency.

'Ask a neighbor or someone to watch them. Hurry,' he will say.

You'll sense there's no time or need for questions and immediately ask the neighbor to watch the kids while you jump into your car and call him back right away.

'What's wrong?' you will ask.

'Something's happened to your dad. You need to get to the house.'

You will begin to feel sick to your stomach, and your heart will feel like it's going to jump out of your chest as you say, 'Just tell me he's alive.'

Flashbacks from just a few weeks ago will rip through every cell in your body.

'No, he's not,' he'll say, his voice cracking.

You'll speed to their house, and within ten minutes, you'll be parked in that familiar driveway, staring at the neighbors standing outside, the house sitter holding their dog, Beau, on a leash, and you'll not only go into shock, but you'll go into that familiar, laser-focused, 'been here before' mode.

The paramedics will be there, and the next thing you'll feel is anger, but anger won't matter anymore because there's no one to blame. It just is.

They'll say to you, 'It must have been a heart attack or aneurysm because he died before he hit the floor. He's in the house, face down on the marble, but his arms are by his side, which tells us he didn't have time to brace himself before he was gone. He died before he hit the floor. Do you want us to have an autopsy done, ma'am?' they will ask.

Inside your head, you'll scream, 'Are you fucking kidding me?'

You'll feel angry, broken, and defeated. You'll yell, 'No, there's no point! Everyone's dead!'

Right at that moment, you'll remember the warning I gave you with your mom, the warning to be careful what you let your eyes see. You'll refuse to go into the house and see him that way. I'm so proud of you for taking care of yourself, Leigh. Mom would be so proud of you.

It's going to be hard enough when you go in there after his body has been removed. You'll see the hole in the sheetrock about the *size of a softball where his head hit the wall before his body landed on the floor.*

As you look closer, you'll see hair caught in the broken pieces of sheetrock, and somehow, that tiny detail will make it so painfully real for you.

Leigh Anne, I need to warn you that when you look up from the floor where he was found, you'll see the large portrait of yourself that Mom loved so much that she displayed it on the wall. It'll be hanging just a few feet directly above the hole in the sheetrock, and it will look eerily like somewhat like a headstone to you now.

I'm proud of you, though. You'll go into autopilot and start taking care of business. You'll autodial the funeral home to ask for his body to be picked up by the morgue. You'll be familiar with how this end-of-life process works by now.

At some time during those moments, you'll add a few more masks to wear as a survival tactic.

You won't be aware of this consciously, but you'll progress deeper into flight or fight or survival mode. I'll warn you, though, that living in fight or flight mode long-term will wreak havoc on your health later in life.

Warning.

Listen, Leigh—you are allowed to grieve. You are allowed to be sad, angry, happy, or any of the above.

Own it, Leigh.

Once you finally reach the doctor on call to have the body released, it will be time. You'll watch the stretcher go into the house, and you'll try to close your ears.

Leigh Anne, whatever part of your heart is still intact is about to be ripped into pieces, but it's the only sense of closure you'll have at the moment. You watched the gurney roll Mom out through the front doors nine weeks and two days ago when you refused to let go of her, but you'll still feel like this is one big nightmare, and in a strange way, you'll still hope she'll come driving up, wondering what in the world was going on at home.

If only it was all one bad dream, and you're going to wake up soon.

You suddenly hear the all too familiar sound of wheels going down the flagstone steps.

Two front wheels, then the two back wheels.

Two front, two back.

That sound will become 'the sound of death' from now on. You'll find yourself going through the exact same process of letting go of the physical body, in a sense, because you'll find yourself standing in the same patch of grass of the front yard, straining your eyes to follow the taillights of the hearse as far as you can see until it disappears in the dark. This will be the only semblance of closure you'll have.

Don't be caught off guard when you realize it's the same hearse that took Mom away.

It's at that moment that you'll collapse right there on the sidewalk.

You're going to feel weak, angel, and the sense of loss, void, shock, and disbelief will be stronger than you.

*Here's the reality, Leigh: you're going to see the world in a completely different way. You'll be uncertain as to **who you are, where you are, and why you're here**. You'll begin to distrust the world you live in because the very foundation you came from will now be completely ripped out from under you.*

*The only two things you are certain of are one, that you love Dylan and Leigh with all of your heart, and you'd lay your life down for them; and two, that your Strength and Faith have carried you this far, and they are the only **things** you'll trust.*

You'll find yourself walking up to the podium to honor your dad as you deliver the eulogy, but it's going to all be very surreal.

For a brief few seconds, you'll look at the guests in the pews and feel as if you're having an out-of-body experience because you just delivered the eulogy for Mom, looking at your dad in the front pew.

You'll snap back to the present moment and continue to read aloud, honoring your dad before you return to your familiar seat in the front pew that will feel cold, breezy, and empty.

Only you and Greg will be sitting in the front pew.

This time.

You'll be gathered around the familiar burial site as you'll watch his matching casket lowered into the ground next to a heaping pile of fresh dirt approximately two to three feet high.

The mound of dirt is where Mom was buried only a few weeks ago.

You'll look around to see the guests looking completely speechless. No one will believe this is real life. Your life. Your brother's life. It's a tragedy that'll leave everyone in shock.

Many of the guests — who will be your family or your parents' friends — will comment on your unwavering strength, Leigh. They'll be familiar with your nickname, Sunshine, and remind you how much Mom and Dad loved you.

Your strength will become your 'superpower,' but once again, Leigh, I'm cautioning you about the unobtainable goal of being 'perfect' — 'P' equals 'Pain.'

Here you sit, Leigh. The words your mom whispered are still crystal clear, but you seem to be so overwhelmed with grief and loss that you can't comprehend them.

You now carry around with you the expectation that you will be 'okay' by now because you're strong, right? You'll add that to the belief you have that if you love someone, it will be painful. They will also die. Loving someone means pain. Pain and death become one in your mind, Leigh.

The finality of it all will be palpable. You'll develop a reoccurring nightmare with the same dark, heavy, strong figure racing toward you as it picks up speed. You'll feel and hear your pulse racing in your sleep. Just as this horrifying figure is about to crush your entire being, you wake up, asking the same question every time:

Why didn't your dad ever tell you that he loved you?

Leigh Anne, your dad was so proud of you in every way, even though you never heard those words.

Again, Leigh, you are loved. Unconditionally. You are worthy and deserving of happiness, love, and peace.

The only way to allow yourself to rise from your own ashes, Leigh, is to be vulnerable as hell, show your wounds, and allow scars to develop.

Burn the suffocating masks.

Yes, you're a single mom, and I don't blame you one bit for putting all of your time and focus into Dylan and Leigh now, but I'm forewarning and reminding you once again.

IF you put off fulfilling the promise you made to Mom as she took her last breath, you'll find yourself in a world of self-sabotage, self-doubt, rebellion, chronic fatigue, emptiness, and not knowing who you are, existing inside of the four walls that protect your heart from the pain of someone you love dying only to exist inside of shame and guilt.

It is the guilt of not fulfilling your promise.

You'll live another decade or two in fear. You'll experience fear of abandonment, rejection, acceptance, people pleasing, food restriction and excessive exercise, body image issues and dysmorphia, self-destructive behaviour... the list goes on, only to find yourself battling a handful of 'incurable' diseases.

Plural.

It will take its toll on your heart, lungs, and liver. It will take 15 years, a global pandemic, and all of the health obstacles to finally decide it is time to Drop the Fucking Mask, Leigh. Stop caring about what others think of you and fulfill the damn promise you made!

Before it's too late for you to do it.

You have a choice, Angel.

Choose wisely.

As you'll know all too well, tomorrow is not promised. Even this next sentence I'm about to write to you is not promised.

Time can only be spent; it cannot be saved.

You still have time to be seen in this world, come out of that suffocating shell, and avoid experiencing a slice of hell.

I love you dearly,

Leigh Anne, My Sunshine

How did the event change my life?
I spent a decade and then some living in fear of death and the fear that everyone I let into my heart was going to 'die on me.' I decided that I needed to be as strong and independent as possible in every aspect of my life. I committed to absorbing and perfecting (to the best of my ability) everything I could possibly think of, everything from how to change a flat tire to all of the financial decisions to be made for the future of my kids and I. I never wanted to rely on or depend on anyone in life because of my all-consuming fear.

Going through the death of someone I love again remains inconceivable, but the difference now is that I can see (and have the evidence) that my level of resiliency is equal to the extent of how honest I am with myself when it comes to my emotions. If I am willing to honor my emotions, my future has endless possibilities that are no longer blocked by walls. Regardless of the inevitable fact that we'll all come to the end of our lives, I'm now capable of living and not just existing. I'm able to make an intentional decision each day to show up in my own life, raw, real, and vulnerable. I choose to live that way in the hope of creating a safe space for someone else to do the same.

What lessons did you learn?
One of the biggest lessons I learned is that I have control over how I perceive the world, and that perception is reality. I've uncovered many deeper layers of myself due to adversity. Somewhere, deep inside, I knew that if I was going to rise from the depths of my despair, it was going to require more of me, more than what I thought I knew or had within.

In a sense, it was as if each layer I discovered and disrupted led me closer to the purity of who I was meant to be and the purpose I was meant to serve in this world. There's an entirely different energy that came with possibilities that I only discovered after I'd fought through the layers of life that had covered up my true sense of self at my core. In a nutshell, I went through hell fighting for the woman I hadn't met inside, only to find her and realize that she was exactly the woman I had hoped to be someday. I now know that I have a choice: I can choose to stuff down my feelings and experience more pain or deal with them by allowing myself to feel all of my emotions.

What would you tell other people experiencing this?
You are meant to be here, no matter how far down your rock bottom might be. I know what it feels like to lose hope or wonder if you matter in this world anymore, but I can say with complete confidence that if you're reading this right now, that thought doesn't get to exist anymore. Looking back, I can count how many lives I must have because, according to science, I shouldn't be here. I'm not alone in these statistics, but it was hard for me to see my worth at times when my perception was so clouded with pain, shame, and more pain. Although we've never met, my hand is reaching out to yours through the words I've written here. All you need is just one hand to grab onto, and if you feel like there's no one in your life reaching down to help you up, I hope you'll remember the story I shared here and envision my hand reaching out for yours.

What are some of the things you would have changed about that situation if you could have?
The times I allow myself to look back over my life, I've literally been brought to my knees. It's because of the overwhelming gratitude I have for the grace and mercy I've been given and the second, third, fourth, and so on chances with which I've been blessed. If I could go back in time, I'd make one crucial change: I'd do the hard work to get to the root of the pain I was carrying around inside so I could be the person I am today. The person I am today wants to help the person I used to be that's stuck in a hopeless state of despair and needs to know she is worthy, needed, and deserves to know what it feels like to love and be loved.

Any final words?

(Excerpt from the recent eulogy I wrote for the passing of my grandmother)

In the end...
What really matters in life?
LOVE.
Love Matters.
In all forms.
All forms, Unconditional Love.

Get messy in life. Everyone has a story. Stories are a gift born from struggles. Ditch the labels and refuse to be put in a box. Take risks and slide into home plate.

No. Matter. What.

How can people get in touch with you and see the work you do?
www.dropthemask.co

The Lotus Self

Romy Brooks, MSc

Integrative Therapist and Coach in Positive Psychology, Autism and Embodiment. Clinical Hypnotherapist. Creative Workshop Facilitator & Trainer, Lecturer, Author, Actress, Artist, Mum and Faerie (mostly on weekends)

What are you passionate about and how are you contributing to the world?

I am passionate...about learning and inspiring the love of learning in others; passionate about how we connect, communicate and interact in the different areas of our lives and how a small change can make a big difference. I am passionate about love, strength, shadows, and the creative courage needed to live our most authentic selves.

Within my differing fields of practice, I have found that being seen, being heard, feeling known, and feeling accepted has a huge impact on our sense of Self, our well-being, and how we then engage within the world.

The simplicity of acknowledgement cannot be underestimated, and its positive impact can be experienced within parenting, relationships, work environments and society.

Describe a pivotal moment you wish to share.
There have been many pivotal moments in my life. Sometimes, we may not realise the significance of them, as they can be a collection of decisions made, choices taken, and roads less travelled that lead us to that clearing in the woods where we face ourselves.

My clearing in the woods was my decision to end my 23-year marriage, and in doing so, I had to face my fears and weaknesses, my cowardice and courage, my incompetency and my strengths.

I had been a romantic, idealistic 22-year-old when we started dating, and within eight months, we had bought a house together and were engaged. A lifetime ensued, full of joy and heartache, laughter and pain, and hope and love. We both tried to heal our family pain through each other's love. I had grown from a child to a woman in our relationship, and that was a hard transition to navigate for both of us. Sometimes, the growth we need is apart from each other, and there are some wounds that need to be healed alone. He was my best friend and then the enemy within. I needed to know myself, own myself, and accept all parts of myself, and that was a journey home.

The courage needed to take that dark journey came from the confidence and learning that grew over the years of my marriage, in the meeting of a man who questioned and challenged my perceptions and beliefs and stayed present with me, and from the love I had for my children. I remember the night I gave birth to my son and laid awake all night watching him. It was the most excruciating sensation of excitement, rapture, awe, and immense love travelling in waves through my body, and I kept whispering, 'I made that.' There was a sense of disbelief in the enormity of such a miracle, and that sense of awe in him has only increased as he has grown into the man he is.

When I first held my daughter, I remember the soft weight of her body on mine and our heartbeats breathing together. Even through the exhaustion, I felt an overwhelming protectiveness that rose fiercely within me when the nurse took her from me to allow me to rest. I could not fully believe in the expansiveness of love until I had my daughter and felt the love I had for my son expand.

Now I believe there is no end to love, no limits, no boundaries, no restrictions. Our hearts know no bounds. It is our perception and the desire that someone else meet our expectations of what we believe love to be that creates a limit to what love is. The love I felt for my daughter was in the awesome miracle of her being, and the love I feel now is in awe of who she is. I now recognise the contraction of love I feel is because I am in fear of its loss.

Based on the wealth of knowledge, wisdom and experience you have now, what would you have liked to say to yourself back then?

Dear Romy,

I didn't realise how difficult I would find writing this letter. There is so much I want to say to you. I wish I had written to you sooner. I wish I had known how to love you sooner.

I am sorry, little one. I love you.

I've written letters of acknowledgement and gratitude to others in the past, but I have not acknowledged you in the same way.

You never deserved to be left out, ignored, or made to feel insignificant by anyone and especially not by me.

How can I expect others to see you if I choose not to see you myself? I see you.

I know your heart is raw with a sense of deep loss. So much of how we measure success comes from what we have, and you have stepped into a scary place of nothingness, letting go of every identity you believed yourself to be, and you feel an emptiness. Stay with that emptiness for a while, and do not fear stepping into the darkness, for you will find much of who you are there, waiting to be loved back into wholeness again.

I am proud of you.

It is not a pride of achievement, success, or perfection. It is the pride of acknowledging yourself as worthy of love, care, and protection and having the courage to own that acknowledgement even when it means stepping into uncertainty, insecurity, and the unknown. This is where trust, faith, and hope live, alongside the courage it took to get you here.

You've built a beautiful, loving home for your family and spent 23 years filling it with laughter, love, and affection...but you forgot about yourself in all of that giving. Your inner child, at last, felt safe and loved, but you are a woman, and that woman is one of passion, desire, creativity, rage, need, and a fierce love that craves expression and acknowledgement. She is significant, and you cannot deny, ignore, or neglect her. She deserves to be loved.

Your heart will break with the choices you make, but it will be a necessary opening for you to heal and love the little girl you once were and become the woman that you are.

Forgive yourself as you forgive others. We are all learning, and we are all loving in the best way we can.

From an early age you learnt the importance of meeting others' needs. It was how you grew to see so deeply into others.

Your childhood was like the neglected adventure playground in Battersea Park; you needed to develop special skills and strengths to navigate its sharpness, its adventure, its opportunities, and its dangers.

Maybe that is why you feel as if you need to learn more, know more, and be more, but you have all the skills you will ever need. You've had the best teachers without realising the lessons they were teaching. You grew up in an environment where you balanced poverty-shame and hunger with the opulence of wealth. You saw childhood neglect in both worlds of rich and poor, experienced abuse, and saw the results of domestic violence. You formed deep friendships that have lasted a lifetime and enjoyed running free and exploring abandoned houses. You have had the best training in how to grow resilience, responsibility, and fairness with kindness, creativity, and hope.

There have always been blessings around you, and you will see them as such once again.

I love you in all your present brokenness, through your brokenness, and because of it... Your brokenness is an illusion. It is only the outer shell that cracks when we are brave enough to break through.

Life can be a strange and confusing place at times. People create so many rules they choose not to follow, and they say such contradictory things that make no sense. It is a place where people deny themselves whilst trying to live as someone else in hiding.

How were you expected to navigate this strange land with so many nonsensical variables?

There were certain things that made sense to you, and you held tightly to them. One of them was the love of your brother. When you questioned everyone else's love, you never needed to question his—it was the two of you against the world. You comforted him through his nightmares, you protected him from bullying childminders, and you fell asleep holding hands. You both grew up with a deeply protective care for each other.

You ignited each other's imagination with your stories and dreams, and this closeness would grow. You were confident in his love, strength, and protection. He will be a guiding light for a lot of your life, but there will come a time when you will both need to step away from each other, and this will be excruciatingly painful, but you will survive.

An inner warrior will surface. She is there to honour your truth, to protect values you hold as integral to your being, and who is fierce in her compassion. She grew silently in the wake of intimidation and shaming, belittling and humiliation, justice, kindness, and hope.

I want you to know that your kindness will touch the lives of many. Chance encounters and deep conversations with strangers are just a drop in the ocean that connects us all.

You see people even when they cannot see themselves. You acknowledge them. They have significance. They are significant. They matter and have a meaning, a reason and a purpose in just being. In a world where there is much visibility, there are millions of invisible people.

I love you, and the tears falling as I write this is because my heart is overflowing, and I wish I could hold you tightly and whisper the reassurance I know you will need and search for in your life, but I am aware that your search is a part of your path, Romy, and your loss, sadness, and the ache of not belonging are a part of your compassion and the kindness you will wrap others in, for that is your way.

You are a gentle soul, and some will see this gentleness as a weakness to exploit for their own gain without realising that you see them quite clearly and that your gentle kindness is showing them another way. You are not responsible for whether they choose that way or not, although there will be times when you feel this is your responsibility. This will be a part of your learning, the boundary of what is yours and what is other. This will be an ongoing lesson, and you will learn it incrementally, for you sense the connectedness of all things in a way that makes boundaries feel almost irrelevant, but they are not, and they are much needed. We each have a reality in which we live, and it is important for you to learn that they are all different. People will be drawn to you for many different reasons, and not all of them are good.

You have such a loving heart and a fierce belly, and you will never shy away from the defence of the vulnerable, a fight for justice and compassion, or the freedom to be heard as you have learnt the importance of feeling acknowledged.

Forgive yourself for the anger and pain you have held onto and the shame and guilt you have felt because of the anger; it is time to let it go. Love is a sensed feeling, an expression, an action, an innate belief, and a soul's truth. You are loved, Romy. This can be very different from feeling loved, but accepting the truth that you are can help alleviate the pain that you're not.

There will come a time when you will live as an adult with your mum. This will not be easy. Unhealed wounds will re-open, but now you will see her through the eyes of a wounded mother, trying desperately to make ends meet and only having the capacity to focus on the practicality of living. You will understand your mother's fear in a way you never could as a child, and you will see her as a woman like you, making different choices and living with the pain of them. Your heart will break open for the love she never received and so desperately wanted.

There will come a time when you will care for your father, and you will see his aggression, rejection, and judgement for the fear and vulnerability that it is and not as a reflection of your not being good enough. You haven't realised how deeply you internalised that judgement. There will be a moment of realisation that you have spent a good part of your adulthood deferring the pain you felt from your dad onto your mum, as you could not cope with the feelings of childhood abandonment at the time. It was never about you.

In those moments, you will see your parents as the beautifully flawed, perfectly human, vulnerably scared people they are, and you truly love them.

P.S. This does not make them less infuriating at times or easier to live with!

They gave you the gift of life and the first set of cards to be played. You loved playing Dungeons and Dragons as a child. With each mission, you had the opportunity to acquire new skills, equipment, strengths, and magic potions, and to make friends, overcome challenges, achieve goals, fail, and learn from it to emerge ready for another adventure.

You will come to realise the strength of a courageous heart and the importance of stepping into those places of discomfort, uncertainty, and fear. They are in simple moments of truth, as in being both challenged and challenging a loved one when you fear rejection or abandonment. There will be moments when your fear stops you from opening up and you will learn through the consequences that follow, the importance of bravery. It is only in these small moments of vulnerable truth that you can live like the person you are, and that person may look very different from the portrayal of the success you see all around you. At times, you will feel so lost and so small as you stand alone with nothing but yourself, watching as people walk away.

I will keep you safe. I will love you.

I want you to know that your shyness will never stop you from defending others. When you are 13, you will even start a petition gathering over 100 signatures for the removal of a bullying teacher.

You show enormous courage as you stand up in front of the class, blushing crimson and pledging to put a stop to the bullying.

At 17, you have the opportunity to apply to be a foreign exchange student to study in a high school in America. With no Internet or mobile phones, you will travel 3,340 miles to live with a host family for a year. This will be one of the turning points in your life. You will experience daily hugs and physical affection that will help you to realise just how important touch is for your well-being, sense of belonging, and self-worth. You will climb a 40-foot ladder to a platform to sing the national anthem acapella at an American football game, although you are petrified of heights and knowing that the last time you climbed a ladder was as a 12-year-old in PE, and you froze halfway up, and the teacher had to rescue you! You will be offered a contract from a recording studio in Nashville and although unable to pursue it, this will give you the confidence to enter singing competitions and apply to drama school when you return to England. You will experience religion for the first time. It will be intoxicating and dangerous and will result in police guards outside of your hospital room with a court order to prevent church members from coming near you. This does not deter your faith or deep connection to God, but rather, it amplifies your own personal relationship without the need for approval or permission from any establishment.

You will stand firm in your principles, even when a teacher humiliates you in front of the class because you refused his advances, when others belittle you as frigid because you refuse to curtail to the 'casting couch' mentality. Their anger and contempt fuel you in future years to look more closely into sexual shame as an ancestral pattern, as a collective strand, and as a genetic hardwiring. This, too, will take courage to speak of, and my dear girl, you have courage!

This letter is different from what I thought I would write to you, but it is what you need to hear right now, as I know you are struggling to find the courage to walk another path. You want to live, but there have been moments when you fight the impulse to die, and the shame you feel for sinking into a well of self-pity is overwhelming at times. Romy, it is not self-pity. You have never stopped to give yourself the compassion you give to others. You are allowed to feel sad without it being labelled depression. You are allowed to feel grief without it being labelled depression. You are allowed to feel anger without it being labelled depression.

Remember the times when you stepped into your courage when you were filled with passion and life. You followed the feelings in your body, not the ruminations and voices in your head that have always kept you stuck.

Breathe out any need for comparison. Right now, your circumstances are so very different and overwhelming compared to what you have experienced over the last 28 years, but the last 51 years have taught you well, and you have all of the creative resources you need to create another way of life, one you can dream into reality.

You have yourself, your knowledge and wisdom, your kindness and passion, your love and freedom, and your creative ideas. Your creative ideas have inspired businesses, projects, and university dissertations! You have brought laughter and acceptance into areas laced with shame, and you have shown great strength in sharing your vulnerabilities.

You are, as we all are, a drop in the ocean, but without those drops, there is no ocean, and that is why you see the value in each drop.

Your daughter's diagnosis of autism at the age of three created another lesson that later led to a deeper understanding of your own struggles and of those around you. You will become an advocate for families and will take on the education system, send letters to MPs and the prime minister, challenge family prejudice, and reframe what it means to be autistic.

You will work with vulnerable families through a pandemic whilst completing an MSc, moving three times and going through a divorce. It will be the separation from your children that will be the hardest to cope with. You could not prepare yourself for a goodbye you never knew was coming. You could not have foreseen being made homeless during a pandemic, and the temporary six months you believed it to be grew into over two years.

There are certain strengths that we cannot teach our children with our presence but only in our absence. You grew those strengths in childhood and wished to protect your children from those experiences for as long as possible. You have watched them navigate the past five years with compassion, understanding, and wisdom that belies their age. You have felt their strength, independence, resilience, and confidence grow.

It is you who now needs to grow, trusting that they have everything they need within themselves to flourish without you.

If I could spare you from things that I know are coming, would I?

As any parent wishes to save their child from pain, my eyes are wet with the tears of knowing that this is not the way, as to do so would be a great disservice to your beautiful soul. Even now, you are teaching me how to parent my own children as I write this to you.

Without these moments, you would not have the strength needed to love others through their brokenness until they can love themselves...

It is okay to make mistakes. It is okay to fail.

It is necessary and needed, and I love you even more for it. Mistakes and failures are a privilege, freedom, and celebration you were never allowed as a child — smile and dance through them now.

You will always value others more than things, and yet you will struggle with valuing yourself until this moment. Until this time.

As I write this, I feel your worth in every fibre of my body in a way that I never have before. You are a gold I never truly appreciated until now.

One day, a little nine-year-old will walk into a classroom wearing the most magnificent turquoise wool coat. It will have fake black fur cuffs and collar and big brass buttons, and she will feel beautiful, regal, and rich in that moment. And even though the other children will point, laugh, and tease you for your second-hand coat, you will go on to inspire others with your eclectic style and non-conformist ways, your courage to stand alone, your courage to stand up, and your courage to be.

Looking back, what made it such an important part of your journey?
I think my divorce was the beginning of my shattering. This breaking apart allowed the space for me to see how entangled and enmeshed 'I am' was with everyone else.

Who am I if I am not who I have always believed myself to be — a daughter, a sister, a wife, a mother? Am I only those things until I am not, and then what am I?

I believe we sometimes hold on too tightly to something we love, and we throttle the life out of it. I think this is true in a lot of different types of relationships. It's a bit of a dramatic way of putting it, but sometimes, we cannot see our own patterns and those of others until it gets to the extreme stage. It doesn't have to be that way. Within relationships, we can choose to grow together and work on our own issues individually and in unison, but it takes two people courageous enough to be vulnerable with each other to enable this to happen. We each come to that courage and our own vulnerability at different stages of our lives when we are ready to. This was a lesson for me. No matter how much you may want something, you have to allow it to be itself, and sometimes, that means walking away from everything you have loved, so it doesn't become something you grow to hate. I loved and appreciated my life, but only when it changed could I learn to see and appreciate things so much more in their absence. The loss and grief grew my gratitude once I had let go of the disappointment and pain.

Does this mean I have regret? How can I? For then, I wouldn't have learnt, and I wouldn't have had love and life. Could I have done things differently? Of course, but then the learning would have been different. We do not learn in isolation from each other, and my pain could be someone else's happiness. We do not always see the beauty of the tapestry we are creating when we work in detail with a few threads.

I can just be myself and trust that is all I ever need to be.

How did this event change your life?
It was my big bang moment. It activated my greatest paradoxical fear: abandonment and nothingness vs entrapment and everything.

I realised that there is a huge difference between attachment and connection. With attachment, there is an element of fear, even if it is a 'healthy attachment'. My children and I had to leave our rented accommodations during the COVID pandemic and couldn't find anywhere to live. They moved in with their father, and I moved into a room at my mum's. The separation was unbearable because of our fear, loss, sadness, and attachment. I believe we are taught attachment rather than connection. With connection, there is trust and love. Connection and trust are living vulnerabilities. It takes a lot of courage to live that way, and sometimes my courage falters. It can be very lonely.

I am vulnerable. I am sad. I am lonely. I am scared. I am passionate. I am creative. I am hopeful. I am curious. I am playful. I am becoming.

What lessons did you learn?
No matter how much you love someone—your children, your partner, your family—if you are not able to show yourself the same kindness, love, and compassion you show others, there will come the point when your ability to give love will dry up as you will have forgotten how to receive it and inadvertently block others from loving you.

NO, can be the most life-affirming, gracious word in your vocabulary. It's how and when we use a word, not what that word is.

I have the courage for those uncomfortable conversations and the confidence to know the truth of my intentions.

We teach by our actions, not just with words, and I believe the blessings of action come from owning our mistakes and seeing failure in the light of a courageous moment of uncertainty and curiosity that doesn't quite go to plan. The blessing comes from choosing to dance with the uncertainty.

What would you tell other people experiencing this?
Be kind to yourself and have compassion for the struggles of those around you. Set a boundary for what and how you allow yourself to experience these things right now. Our capacity to experience people and events in a healthy way varies depending on our capacity to nurture ourselves. In those moments when you feel as if you are going to be overwhelmed, DO something you enjoy: a walk in nature, a hug, watch a comedy, listen to music, dance like no one's watching, paint, garden, go for a drive or ride, swim, fish, run, play sports, or cook. We all need a healthy balance of doing and being.

Acknowledge what your responsibility is, and do not take on someone else's as this can slow down both of your healing.

'Judge not, lest ye be judged.' I've found that when I judge others, I am secretly judging myself, and when I am judging myself, I am priming myself for judging others. Judgement and discernment are two different things. I have recently come to a deepening understanding of this on a practical level through working with Positive Intelligence founder, Shirzad Charmine. Discernment is acknowledging a situation and/or circumstance as it is and feeling an element of empathy for the pain within it before looking at ways to address the issues with kind honesty.

Judgement feels heavy with the need to be right, to prove someone else wrong, to fear that you're not good enough, and the need to validate yourself, justify, excuse, blame, shame and criticize.

Let judgement go. Learn with discernment and live with kindness.

You are loved, x.

What are some of the things you would have changed about that situation if you could have?
There are things I wish I had handled better. Moments I wish I had stepped into courage sooner, but I did not because I did not have these resources in me at that time. They grew through the struggles, life experiences, and losses I had.

Any final words?
'Out beyond the ideas of wrongdoing and right doing,
There is a field. I'll meet you there.
When the soul lies down in that grass,
The world is too full to talk about.
Ideas, language, even the phrase
'each other'
Doesn't make any sense.
The breeze at dawn has secrets to tell you.
Don't go back to sleep.
You must ask for what you really want.

Don't go back to sleep.
People are going back and forth
Across the doorsill
Where the two worlds touch.
The door is round and open.
Don't go back to sleep.'
Rumi.

How can people get in touch with you and see the work you do?
www.romybrooks.com

Hanging onto Hope

Tiffany Brix

Entrepreneur & Wellness Consultant

What are you passionate about and how are you contributing to the world?
Having overcome many autoimmunity challenges since I was a child and celebrating several important milestones including reversing liver cirrhosis due to autoimmune liver disease, a milestone that many, even in the medical field, still believe is impossible, I am passionate about bringing hope to the world through my inspiring healing journey. I fully understand the hopelessness that so many people experience with chronic health issues, as they battle with debilitating fatigue and brain fog, common with autoimmune issues. My mission as a wellness consultant is to lead people to take back control and responsibility for their own wellness, use tools to empower the individual, *anti*-age gracefully, and explore a path toward a better quality of life.

Describe a pivotal moment you would like to share.
I deal with autoimmune issues. My body attacks itself in silent and invisible ways. I look healthy and vibrant, even when I can barely

make it through the day. Fatigue, brain fog, and a deep feeling of hopelessness are the most stubborn symptoms. Autoimmune issues are often silent and invisible, and I've dealt with them for most of my life. I've been at least 30 years younger than other patients in the waiting room. I've had doctors shrug their shoulders, say there is nothing else they can do, and dismiss my pleas to try something, anything, to help me feel better. I've left doctors' offices in tears. I've left feeling like a faceless medical chart where the numbers of my lab results and lists of prescriptions were all they saw. I've felt hopeless, like a burden, as if things couldn't get better. I've felt like giving up.

However, I haven't let any of these events be the final answers for me. The determination to find better answers started in my life before I even have a memory of it. It started before I could crawl. My legs weren't developing normally, and one was crooked. They tried casts and corrective braces with little success. The doctors expected I would never walk without corrective assistance. Even so, my parents had faith that better answers would arise, and arise they did. A chiropractor in a small town in South Georgia not only had an idea of what was causing the problem in my legs, but he also had experience with it. He said it was an air bubble in my brain, and a series of gentle inversion treatments had the best chance of correcting it. The braces and corrective shoes came off, and after a few sessions of swinging me upside down by my ankles, my legs straightened. The results, compared to the treatment, seemed to defy logic. What happened seemed miraculous.

My parents saw with their own eyes how there could be better answers and more successful results. They saw how uncovering the actual cause of an issue could lead to better treatments. What happened was a miracle they could see with their own eyes. So, when invisible illnesses started attacking my body, they already had the faith that things would be okay. When, over a decade later, doctors dismissed my mom's request to check my thyroid—they thought I was too young to have that problem—she persisted. Again, a few years later, when I was 15 years old, liver biopsies came back with shocking amounts of cirrhosis due to autoimmune liver disease. The doctor pulled my parents aside and told them not to expect a long life for me, yet my parents believed there would be more hopeful answers and better-than-expected outcomes. They did not tell me the grim prognosis because they didn't believe it would be my truth, and they didn't want to invite that possibility into my reality.

Looking back, what made it such an important part of your journey?
For many years, I stayed fairly stable in my health. I had enough momentum to coast along with the status quo. Then, after an especially stressful year when I was 35, I received yet another autoimmune liver disease diagnosis. I felt too sick to hold onto much hope. Considering that cirrhosis was already present for at least 20 years, I didn't see how I could make it another 20 more. Even that length of time seemed to be on the heavily optimistic side—I wouldn't even be 60 years old yet. I honestly didn't think I would make it long enough to see my kids graduate high school. I barely had the energy to walk across the room. My body ached. I had bouts of disturbing brain fog. I'd already been fighting against my body for my whole life, and I didn't have much fight left.

Then something shifted. It started out as the motivation just to feel okay enough to enjoy a couple more years with my kids. I wasn't trying to extend my life. I was just trying to be able to enjoy the few years I thought I had left as much as possible. Yet small miracles kept happening that changed my expectations. During this time, social media was growing and changing. While social media platforms have plenty of negatives, they connected me with information that, I can say with certainty, saved my life. I found better answers. I found physicians who were championing better options for their patients with alternative therapies. I found medications that gave me more effective results and doctors who were willing to listen to me and treat me outside of the box. I found deeper truths. I found a fire inside of myself to fight for a better quality of life. I took control of my wellness. I took control of my prognosis.

I didn't fully realize until recently that my healing journey had started so early in my life. The pattern of not accepting the initial medical answers given started when that small-town chiropractor held me upside down and swung me by my ankles. My world literally and figuratively has flipped upside down so many times. The answers seemed to be waiting for me to turn the norms on their head as well.

When I was just a few months old, I was physically flipped upside down. The physician executed this with care and purpose. Over the years, I have instinctively returned to flipping upside down through physical inversions. These twists into the upside-down have many healing benefits. You can't help but gain new or different perspectives. That first foray onto the road less traveled, when my parents chose the alternative treatment, sent the rest of my life in a different direction. It showed all who knew my story that the odds of your prognosis are not definitive. It showed that the source of the problem can be somewhere completely different than where the symptoms began and that the body can, in fact, achieve miracles.

When my parents received grave news again when I was 15, I wonder if the moments in the chiropractor's office crossed their minds. I wonder if they remembered the first miracle that had given my body the chance to heal beyond initial expectations. This time, we could not abandon modern medicine. However, my mom didn't take it as an exclusive answer. She found alternative options to try alongside mainstream treatments. Not every answer is as black and white as my first journey into the topsy-turvy.

Sometimes, using both is better.

Sometimes, using both is necessary.

Sometimes, poison is prudent.

Other times, you have to make a choice and jump in with both feet and no safety line.

I believe that the body remembers even when the mind doesn't. That moment of healing, with my head swinging below my feet, ignited a fire within my bones to remember miracles are not only possible, to know that not only am I worthy of miracles, but that miracles would be part of my story. The mind is an integral part of wellness. The most fundamental part of receiving miracles is simply believing that they are possible.

Based on the wealth of knowledge, wisdom, and experience you have now, what would you have liked to say to yourself back then?

Punkin—

Sweet Baby Girl,

Your crooked little legs are bound into forced submission. You feel trapped even though you cannot even speak yet. You are being conditioned to obey and keep your voice quiet. You will be told that your voice of fire makes others uncomfortable and needs to stay inside. You are told you will be broken your whole life, but it won't always be like this. Do not believe when someone says 'you will never...'; they do not know. Even when something is true for everyone else, it does not mean it is true for you. What the world thinks it knows will try to keep you caged. Your legs are trapped just like your fire, but this smoldering will just make it burn even hotter, and it will blaze when it is finally released. You will heal against all odds. In fact, fuck the odds. You are not the numbers. Over and over, you will heal like a phoenix to burn and rise again. You are an example and an observer. You will then share, as a vessel of a prophet, for what is possible. You see the world differently. Some will dismiss your message as heresy. Perhaps, when the chiropractor swings you upside down to straighten your tiny little crooked leg, it sets you on a course for your whole life to form a different perspective, one that anyone can have if they allow themselves to let go of their feet being planted firmly on the ground. At that moment, before you could even walk, you flew. You may forget this early flight for many years, but you will awaken. Your mom lived her example for you. She stepped into faith and stood firmly with the able legs you didn't have yet. She showed her faith for you to heal. It was a healing that she wouldn't be able to give herself at the end of her life, but she still gave you her example, both in action and in caution. She gave you the example to say, 'You don't know what will happen,' when someone doubts you.

Baby girl, your little bald head hasn't even sprouted its head full of curls yet. You were even born on an unlikely day, a day of falling snow in South Georgia, where snowflakes rarely form. You have many unlikely odds on their way to you many times in your life. These odds will try to crash over you like waves. They will try to drown you, squelch you, my beautiful little phoenix, but you will quietly prove them wrong. You will resurface again and again. You will rise up again and again. As many times as you are pushed down, abandoned, or forgotten, you will always triumph. You will continue to find your wings when you think they have burned. Be blind to their looks of pity. Be deaf to their disbelief. You will not only walk, but your legs will, in fact, be one of the strongest parts of you, second only to your will. You will be upside down around the world as you share your healing story. You won't even fully understand the beauty of the synchronicity in the echo from this moment, right now, not until much later.

You, little warrior, will never have the chance to have a normal adult life without health challenges. You will have to fight every step just to feel normal. When you are 12 years old, your mom will know something isn't right. She will fight with doctors because they will say you are too young to have thyroid issues. When you are 15, she will hear grave news about you, that you have autoimmune liver disease, and all of the research she could find leads to terminal answers. Cirrhosis will already be in your still developing body, without a drop of alcohol having touched your lips yet. Then, at 35, you will feel so sick again, barely able to muster the energy to walk across the room, desperate for a place to sit every time you stand. A diagnosis of another autoimmune liver disease will strangle what's left of your hope.

Little girl who will be a woman of quiet strength, you will spend what seems to be too long trying to run from your feminine nature. You will feel like that part of you is weak. You will believe the lies for too long, but don't worry, little one — you will find what you need when you need it. Healing is always on the way. It may sometimes be too late to help the ones you love dearly, and you may not be able to help those who refuse to receive it, but learning that you can't save everyone is a lesson you will have to realize many times. You will learn this on many levels.

You won't believe the rare fire others will see in you, not for a long time. That's how it will have to be to learn the lessons you need. I wish I could protect you from some of these lessons, but I cannot. I know that you have to walk through the darkness. You must become hopeless, so hopeless. You must feel that emptiness and feel alone in order to hear the whispered echo of your deepest voice. You must think that there is no hope left, so you may uncover the gift of hope inside you.

There will be doubters who claim that you spew false hope for others. These are the ones who are scared of hope. They fear hope because hope alone doesn't create change. Hope alone does not create miracles. Hope requires action because it inspires it. Hope is not stagnant. Those who want to silence your message of hope are the ones who fear what hope will ask of them. Healing often requires sacrifices of comfortable cycles.

Punkin, listen closely: you will need both mainstream and alternative therapies. You will need the balance. Just like your legs need to try the braces to know their limitations so you can find what truly works, you will have to embrace a system that doesn't believe you can heal. You will embrace it to learn from it, but it is only a tool to use. You will glean what helps and what is merely a temporary fix or a necessary evil to keep you alive. There will be some who try to control the direction you take, but you will find your own way. Little one, I must warn you that portions of that road will be heartbreakingly lonely. You will long to feel the warmth of encouragement from others, but, my strong little girl, you will be a woman who will muster that encouragement for yourself when you feel all is lost. Then, you will have an overflow of encouragement for others.

You aren't even old enough yet to understand these words I am saying to you. Know that your body remembers more than your mind does. You will have an illogical fear of having your legs restrained, unable to even sleep in a sleeping bag or with both legs under the covers for many years, and you won't make the connection to your crooked leg being in a brace until this moment. Just as your tiny body remembers the confinement, your body will remember these words I tell you now. Your soul and spirit will remember. Time isn't a straight line. You will hear me now, and that will give you a tiny voice to watch how your mom fights for better answers for you. Somehow, what I say now is something you have heard long ago. It is the voice of your ancestors. It is the stubbornness of your lineage. I speak it now for anyone to read, but these words were always and have already been written inside of you.

Little mama, they will say you shouldn't have kids because of the medication you have to take, medicines that are poison but are part of the process to keep you alive. They will tell you this, but don't despair—you have the most wonderful kids on the way to you. They will choose you, imperfect you. Western allopathic medicine will save their lives, as well. I believe that you will have many times when you will fight for additional, alternative options for them that will help them live a better quality of life. You will empower them to pursue their own healing, but just as you had to choose to take the torch from your mom's example, they have their own path to choose. They will have to make the changes and daily choices for themselves.

Baby feminine goddess, you are a canary in the mine. What makes you sick slowly destroys everyone, even if they don't realize it yet.

They just don't know. Many will see you as weak because of your body dysfunctions, but you find a way out. You don't die in the darkness. Very few will recognize your cautionary example. They will think they are not affected. They will not see the connection. They will think that what hurts you won't hurt them because they don't feel it. Yet. Many won't listen to your song of warning as you fly out into the open skies. It's not your job to save everyone. All you can do is heed the sunshine calling to you and sing your song on your way to better skies. Some people just can't hear the music. Some people are too busy shouting their judgement to hear anything else at all. It's not your job to sing louder. When someone is ready, they will hear. They will hear it with their heart.

Beautiful little fighter, you do not fit into a mould. There will be times when others try to get you to fit, to train you like they tried to train your legs. They will try to tell you what will happen to you, but you don't do what's expected. There is a time for you to be a good girl.

Then, you will be a rebellious woman, not to be told what to do.

The most important thing is for you to always fight for the choice to be you, to do you as only you know best. It's what your mom fought to show you by example. She fought for there always to be hope. Do not ever let others take your choice to decide for your health. If you always did only what you were told, you might still be in a body that never walked freely, never did a backbend while balancing on a paddle board in the water, never had children, never healed when too many believed it was impossible. If you had only done what you were told, you might not be here at all. Do not make choices based on what is easier for others to handle or believe. Do not relinquish your autonomy to choose what is best for you. It is your job to put your health first. It is not your job to save everyone. It is not your job to be predictable. It is not your job to make others comfortable at the expense of your wellness. You must always fight for yourself. Healing yourself first is the only way to help anyone else.*

*There will be times when you feel so deeply ordinary. You will feel so average. Full of ideas that never actualize. Buried potential. Remember that you are more than the sum of your parts, my precious fire soul. When you are average, it gives you a humbleness to see from eye level. You do not have to be great to be special. Perhaps you have greatness ahead of you that even I haven't seen yet. I do not know your whole story. Perhaps another, wiser version of myself is speaking to me as **her** younger self to hear her wisdom that I can't yet fathom. Perhaps I am just a part of the fractal conversation with myself over time.*

Little girl, there will be people who want to know why you got to heal and beat the odds, but not them. They will want to discredit your experience because they can't replicate it. You will even question, 'Why me? I'm not special over anyone else.' This is partly true. No, you aren't more deserving than others. You don't deserve a miracle over anyone else, much less multiple miracles, but the question is not for you or anyone else to ask, 'Why me?' Each person must not only ask but believe for themselves in every layer, 'Why NOT me?'

*Perhaps the answers are not in what predictably happens for most people. Perhaps the real answers, the whys, are in the exceptions to the rules. Perhaps the miracles are, in fact, where the answers hide. Maybe the miracles are what is actually supposed to happen. Maybe we need to turn the way we look at it all upside down. Get a new perspective. Maybe instead of asking, 'Why has something different happened to her?' we need to ask, 'What is the obstacle that keeps this from happening to everyone?' Maybe the problem is in what we expect, what we **believe** to be 'normal.'*

So, little Punkin, take the mainstream, well-paved road for a while. Learn what you need for when you blaze that path everyone thinks is impossible. Friends will abandon you. There will be times when it feels like even those who love you just can't understand how it feels to have to work so hard against your own body. There will be times when your path makes others uncomfortable. Whatever their reasons, that is their journey. Recognize the lessons you need to learn and where you need to heal something else within you.

Your journey toward healing started by hanging upside down, little one. Keep hanging upside down every chance you get. Turn the system upside down. Flip the table on the expectations. Make the exception to the rule be what everyone expects. Kick the odds to the curb and lead the way for everyone to receive the miracles that are waiting for them. Your example might help more people start following that little canary out of the mine. If you can make it out, sweet little bird, then why can't they? The possibilities are only real if you believe. So, what will you believe?

How did this event change your life?
I have made it far enough in my journey to know I can't wish away parts of it. I know that, as much as I would like for some of the parts to be different, the sequence of events had to happen the way they did. I had to learn the lessons. I had to know the darkness to fully appreciate the light.

One aspect that I do hope becomes an option in the future is that I wish I could have explored more of my wellness journey *with* my doctors and not *in spite of* my doctors. My allopathic doctors did a wonderful job of keeping me alive to exist another day. They used the tools they knew to get the numbers in my bloodwork to acceptable levels. However, merely existing is a bare minimum. Life is something that is best in quality, not quantity. In my quest for living better, I had to sort through the bad information and even bad science. Wouldn't it be wonderful to feel like my doctors really listened and valued my knowledge and experience? Perhaps that is why I had experienced such a lonely stretch. Maybe my story will be one of many that help change the culture and tide of allopathic medicine. We have to stop treating the parts of a person and understand that emotions are rooted deeply within the body and must be treated integrally. We have to remember that a crooked leg may be because of something going on in the head. Isolating symptoms does not lead to answers. Even isolating the body's systems isn't the answer. We are complex and integrated beings.

What lessons did you learn?
We must take responsibility for our own bodies, minds, and spirits. Don't wait for labs or symptoms to tell you that you are sick. We are

all getting sick. We are all headed down into the mine of disease. Some don't realize it until they are stuck so far below the surface of wellness that they require a massive rescue.

What would you tell other people experiencing this?
Take the wheel of your wellness. Don't wait. Steer it where you want it to go. Find a medical team who will listen to you and take your input seriously. Find a medical team who will consult with you as much as they expect you to consult with them. Don't accept being 'talked at' and told that it is just how it is. And remember that you must also hold onto your responsibility and consider digging for answers that may be buried.

Any final words?
What we believe to be real becomes real in our personal worlds. Our beliefs affect our realities and can even cause changes in our physical bodies. Always, *always* believe in the best outcomes. Believe that any setbacks are leading to something better. While you're at it, start finding miracles that have already happened in your life. Perhaps it's not that you haven't received a miracle yet, but that your definition of a miracle is all wrong. Not all miracles are invisible angels pulling you from the imminent grip of death. Miracles can seem small—a scene in a television show that triggers a sequence of events that changes your life. A miracle can be a social media post by a stranger that you happen to stop and read, and that leads you to better knowledge. A miracle can be feeling so hopeless that your life becomes dark enough for you to see the dim light of a new path. A miracle can even be a chapter in a book you stumbled upon in the

most serendipitous way. It's possible that just changing the filter through which we see our lives can bring incredible changes.

Identify the miracles in your life that have already happened. Feel as if you are already worthy of miracles because they have been happening all along; you just didn't recognize them yet. I have experienced many miracles so far, and I still have more miracles on the way. I still have healing to do. I still have lingering challenges, so I expect miracles to come my way and guide me to even better wellness.

Let's turn the expectations upside down. Let's start expecting miraculous outcomes for everyone, especially for ourselves. Let's all be The Unlikely. What if we just turned the whole system on its head? What if, in turning the way we look at everything upside down, we find where the elusive answers hide?

Let's believe.

Let's turn upside down.

How can people get in touch with you and see the work you do?
www.instagram.com/Tiffanybrix.author

Why I Befriend Fear and Disrupt

Somalía Brown

Disruptor of All things, and Everything concerning you; Wife, Author; Mother to the King of the Spirit Realm, Demon Slayer and Warrior Princess; International Transformational Speaker, Pioneer of the Shift "World ChangHers" that Disrupt and Befriend Fear.

What you are passionate about and how are you contributing to the world?

Interrupting the current flow of your life to cause a paradigm shift in your mind to give you a mindset of dominion that propels you forward.

My mandate: to train and impact millions to become the powerful World ChangHers and DisruptHers of harmful systems; to prevent deaths in relationships, both earthly and spiritual; and to empower those to dismantle the 'old ways of doing things' in life and within their relationship with God. I'm a part of a special forces team that are kingdom disruptors from the womb.

Describe a pivotal moment in your life you wish to share.
On May 31, 2022, you enter your bedroom ready for bed and feel a presence in your room. You immediately know that you will have a spiritual encounter that night. Like clockwork, an angel appears. They lay you on your back, place a finger on your forehead, and say, 'I have something for you.' As you think these words, they are simultaneously transcribed in front of you: 'Do something.' The angel looks at you and assertively says, 'Do Something.' You wake up and hear these words:

'Now you have befriended fear; it's time for you to do something.'

As you have not even conceived or thought about, fear will control you. Fear will overwhelm you, but the tables will turn. You will learn to befriend fear to the point at which it will determine the chess moves of your life. This is a crucial moment in the formation of who you are and who you will become.

Based on the wealth of knowledge, wisdom, and experience you have now, what would you have liked to say to yourself back then?

So, as you are being formed in your mother's womb, Somalia, I want you to hear these words...

You are a disruptor. YOU are a disruptor. Your very presence shifts any atmosphere without you even knowing or trying. You prevent systems, processes, and situations from continuing as usual or as expected. You, at your very core, operate in disrupted thought, which is essentially operating in diverse thinking. You walk in unlimited power from God to influence. Your light unveils darkness that is trying to hide. Wherever you go, a darkness that is overt and disguised must manifest because you are here. Your light disrupts this earth.

Your father carries a powerful sound that shifts any environment he speaks in. He's the epitome of living a disrupted life, someone who is very much against any kind of authority and cannot stand being told what to do. This generational trait will teach you decisiveness, determination, and grit. Your father was told he would not be able to have children; then your brother was born. Your parents wanted a girl; your brother wanted a sister. They prayed in agreement, and here you are. I sent you, their welcome disruption. Your presence disrupts the Earth.

You are born to a lineage of forerunners of independence who are dependent on the power of God. You will walk in a significant power of influence and evolve into a formidable opponent for the kingdom of darkness. You are about to disrupt your mother's birth plan because she's carrying you, and her body can't help but succumb to your significant influence, even from within her.

Your mother walks unconventionally. She's different. Her light shines bright because she disrupts societal norms. Her pregnancy wasn't rough, hard, or traumatic, unlike the stories of many others.

You are just like your mother, never meant to blend in but to stand out. You come from a long line of disruptors who fight for freedom for all.

In the first trimester, your heart is being formed with compassion to walk this life differently. Your brain waves were developing, and as they developed, they were in alignment with the frequency of God and a mindset to disrupt all things and everything around you.

In the second trimester, as your eyes were being constructed and moving to the front of your face, God gave you the special gift to see multi-dimensionally and discern things beyond what they appear to be to the naked eye. As your ears shifted to their place, your hearing was being finetuned to hear God's voice and discern His voice versus the rest. You may not always understand what you hear, but you will come into a knowingness at the right time.

In the third trimester, as you were continuing to grow in size and weight, your lungs were still maturing into a powerhouse to make the sound you will eventually carry. The frequency of what is released from your voice calls things forth, shuts things down, and speaks life over your jurisdiction. Your voice disrupts this earth.

You will be born on time, not in a state/general hospital but in a Jewish hospital. You will be there, so the people I have chosen attend to you and your mother. Also, so that your mother won't be coerced into a c-section, and her wishes will be honored.

Your mother worked for the entire duration of her pregnancy, and as such, you will adopt her gritty, focused, and tenacious nature. Whatever you do as a mom carrying a baby becomes who your children are. As you would have felt, your mother had a strict routine: wake up, exercise, have breakfast at the same place every day, take the bus, take two trains, walk, and sometimes, even run to catch the right bus. Your mother's knack for routine and incredible discipline will be the traits you inherit.

I gave you a mother that operates in Godly principles and a father that operates in world principles. These drastically different experiences will enable you to encounter the perfect balance to see what being different truly looks like.

Never doubt the power of God speaking through you directly to others. The people you work with will be transformed spiritually, physically, mentally, and emotionally simply because they have encountered you. Through you, the World Changers you encounter will be equipped to learn how to be their best selves, manifest their gifts, and operate in their higher forms. The work you will do will transform them and impact not just their immediate circle but their world, which will enable them to manifest God's work. All of these elements will set you in good stead when you do God's work. You will work with women who have voices so powerful that when they speak those things happen. You will help these women understand the gravity of their voices, even if they do not know it yet. You will aid women who can't stand to sit idle and watch injustice happen right before their eyes.

You will work with go-getters who know there is more to this world than what we are being fed. The only problem is that they don't know where to start, so they feel inadequate, misunderstood, and beaten down by the world, and those closest to her have bullied her for her perspective, her voice, her posture, and her outlook on life.

You will meet these types of women so you can do your core work. The work I've put you here to do, your purpose. Your core work is to disrupt the old patterns, and you have been socially curated and socialized primarily by your parents and society. Your core work is to align others with their true selves and empower them to operate in their purposes. You will unlock and uncover what's been hidden and enhance their God-given authoritative voices for the earth to use.

The significant influence you carry is found simply within your presence. Your presence commands attention. When you walk into a room, everything stops, conversations pause, and heads turn. They take you in just because your presence shifts their atmosphere. You are so powerful that it will take you a while to understand your power. You interrupted your mother's plans just by your presence. The ambience of a room changes just because you're there. Your presence disrupts this E.

Always remember who you are in the moments when the darkness stares at you in the face upon arising in the middle of the night, and fear grips your entire soul. Remember who you are. Remember who you are when the world comes against you, saying your skin isn't the correct color, and your hair curls up. Remember who you are when your Spanish accent isn't accepted but ferociously rejected. Remember who you are when you are the only Afro-Latina girl who decided to play coed soccer, and you are neither welcome nor wanted but simply ridiculed.

Remember who you are when your parents say you will have to take confirmation into Catholicism, and your spirit gives you pause. Your spirit disrupts this earth.

Remember who you are when you must choose between the sport you love and the sport you are excellent at to assist the family unit. Your gifts disrupt this earth.

I need you to remember who you are when you are in the second semester of your senior year and you have the biggest decision (choice) to make in your entire life.

Remember who He has called you to become when your gifts—I mean the supernatural, non-earthly gifts—begin to awaken, and you are looked at crazily through the eyes of the world. I want you to remember that you were built for this. You were destined for this. Your dad was strong and rebellious and made sure that things happened on his watch. He guaranteed change, and that, Somalia, runs through your very veins. Your strength disrupts this earth. On the other side, your mom, oh, what can I say? She forged a way where there was no way. She created her own paths, a trailblazer and forerunner in her own right. So, you have no choice but to walk and accept that the very blood that runs through your body is disruptive, but it's been set apart for the kingdom of God. Remember that. As a trailblazer, you disrupt this Earth.

Remember that when you say, 'I do,' your marriage becomes your purpose, and you need to learn to protect it at all costs. Do this by giving it back to God. Your marriage is here to help change other marriages, so keep that at the forefront of your mind.

Remember that when you get pregnant, your three pregnancies are significant in their own rights. Your first pregnancy is where fear will try to engulf you. You will have ghost accidents in which you will see yourself having an accident, but they don't happen in reality. These happenings are designed to disrupt your pregnancy and distract you from preparing, but remember that you are strong. Your firstborn's strength will disrupt your strength. The cesarean you did not want will not stop you from having the vaginal birth you did want with the next two consecutive babies. Take heed to this warning: YOU WILL HAVE TO BEFRIEND FEAR TO HAVE YOUR NEXT TWO CHILDREN.

With pregnancy two, I want you to remember that you will have the opportunity to choose, to say yes or no. Say yes because the blessing this child will bring is far greater than any birthing trauma.

When number three appears, know that he will be the child you didn't know you needed to complete your family. Despite almost losing him and having to fight tooth and nail to birth him naturally, he is destined to be a part of the Brown family.

You are undefeated because of the frequency of love with which you walk. As you walk in love, you disrupt this Earth. The power of God in which you walk will dismantle and disrupt everything containing darkness. You disrupt this Earth. You will understand and walk in the supernatural because you have disrupted life and death. You disrupt this earth. You will have an unshakeable self-belief that will inspire and impact millions because it's abnormal, almost like an anomaly. You disrupt this Earth. Get ready to shift the world as you lead by example with an influence that demands excellence from anyone within reach of your spirit. Your spirit disrupts the Earth. Your very presence shifts any atmosphere without you even knowing or trying.

You disrupt the Earth. YOU are a disruptor.

Looking back, what made it such an important part of your journey?
I have been empowered in a multitude of ways simply by looking back. I realize that it's in my blood to disrupt, and it's not just something I stumbled upon. I'm not just a self-proclaimed disruptor, but it is something that my presence does naturally, as I was able to do it even from within the womb. It was a subconscious act that turned into a conscious and physical act I do everywhere I go.

Retrospectively, the experience of being incubated in the womb was a crucial part of my journey because it was the beginning of who I am, and if I could disrupt at birth, I can only imagine who I will become in my divine life. It enhances my confidence of who I am.

When I signed my life contract, I knew that coming through the birth canal, I would be a disruptor, but unfortunately, when we come through the birth canal, the trauma causes us to forget who we are and what we came here to do.

Reflecting retrospectively made me realize that I was a supernatural baby from the beginning. My mother's birth experience with me reminded me of what I had signed up for, who I was, and who I was sent to be. It reminded me of what I said I would do. It made my story more profound, knowing that my presence alone is enough to disrupt. And it reminded me why I needed to befriend fear because, in the womb, I knew no fear. Fear didn't exist, and I was able to perform my first disruption. Looking back, this has made me realize the importance and the power of befriending fear. I operate in a different dimension because it helps me understand where I'm going and how to maneuver prophetically because I know where I've been.

As I look back, I realize me being a Disruptor is my legacy, and I choose to Pay It Forward to others' lives and when I disrupt their entire world, it's more of an impactful journey for both them and me. My presence as a disruptor is so poignant it cannot be denied, so reflecting made it important because it made me realize the ricochet of the impact of pebbles that can stem from one simple disruption.

How did this event change your life?
I learned that this thing we call life is happening for you, not to you. Everything we encounter, and the situations we face, are to build us into the people we are destined to be. What I was given by having a rebellious father and alternative mother is a bloodline that

doesn't conform. I realized that my disruption of my mother's birth journey activated the supernatural disruptor in me. The fear that followed me—no, that was attached to my life—closely for all of my life would help me understand your fears so I can show you how to befriend them and use them as a confirmation that this is exactly what you are supposed to do.

What lessons did you learn?
Learning that I disrupted my mother's birth and that both of my lineages are natural disruptors took the blinders off of my eyes, and I hope it will help you to see your situation in life in a greater light. I acknowledge that my language and posture as a Disruptor draw you to me to interrupt where you currently are and help you to excel in ways you never knew were possible.

What would you tell other people who might be experiencing this?
I would tell other people who have experienced what I have that they should always look back to gain an understanding of who they are. If I had asked my parents sooner and looked back at the pregnancy earlier, the confidence I have now, knowing that I come from a lineage of disruptors, would have been there long ago. I would tell them to own being a disruptor, own being an alternative, own, accept and act like it's okay, that everywhere you go, you are bound to disrupt the atmosphere, the conversation, the situation, anything, and everything. Being a disruptor is okay when you finally and fully walk into your purpose, and you know what it's for. If you are just learning that everywhere and anywhere you go your presence disrupts something and interrupts anything and you're not sure why it's happening, stop questioning! Pay attention to what you disrupt and interrupt.

I want you to know that you are able to be stretched beyond what you think you can handle. Old paradigms need to be broken down to build you up as the powerful Him or Her you are! After reading this, my goal is to show how what you have or haven't been doing for you, and that your stomach is filled from my chapter and for you to say, 'This is exactly what my soul has been searching for.'

I'm not for everyone, but I am for those who are called and attracted to the sound of my voice, knowledge, experience, and abilities. I look forward to your new era.

Any final words?
Remember that life happens for you, not to you. Everything happens for your own good, whether you can see it at the moment or not. I wouldn't change anything about my past because it would change the trajectory of my life and who I am today. Whatever you do, remember that there is a mindset shift you can experience to see things in a different light. There is always a mindset shift to be had so you can be elevated to a new dimension.

I hope this chapter has disrupted you in some way, shape, or form, as I know it should. Lastly, I was born to disrupt and interrupt any and all noise that stops your mindset from shifting and your movement from progressing forward. Keep shifting with me. Join the movement of disrupting and dismantling the harmful systems around us and the societal norms the world has curated to which we don't belong.

How can people get in touch with you and see the work you do?
Meet me here: www.worldchangher.co

Special Thanks

When putting together a book like this, it is never done alone. There was so much support, help, and encouragement along the journey, and this is a good place to thank so many.

Firstly, a massive thank you to our courageous authors who stepped forward to share their stories in the hope they would positively change someone else's life, overcoming their own fears, trepidations, and beliefs surrounding their experiences. It takes a special kind of person to walk in faith, and this is a part of their destiny and contribution to the world.

Secondly, to our celebrities, who not only went through a similar process to write their notes back to their younger selves but also dedicated their time and energy despite their busy schedules.

Also, thank you to Danni Blechner and her team at Conscious Dreams Publishing for making this process so easy and painless. It truly is an honour to work alongside you again.

Thank you to Jacqueline Freeman for being a constant support to the authors and I during the group writing process.

Last but not least, to all of the previous authors, our friends, families, and supporters—you know who you are—thank you for holding the faith and the mission close to your heart whilst the world shifted and changed.

Kezia Luckett

www.ingramcontent.com/pod-product-compliance
Lightning Source LLC
Chambersburg PA
CBHW060047230426
43661CB00004B/689